HOME
BOAT-
COMPLETION

Ex Libris
John Hall

Buckie Library Sale
Jan 89

By the same author

MANUAL OF POTTERY AND PORCELAIN RESTORATION

HOME BOAT-COMPLETION

A guide for amateurs to fitting out GRP,
ferro-cement, and steel hulls

David Everett

ROBERT HALE · LONDON

Copyright © David Everett 1982
First published in Great Britain 1982

ISBN 0 7091 9480 3

Robert Hale Limited
Clerkenwell House
Clerkenwell Green
London, EC1R 0HT

98193

623.82

Photoset in Great Britain by
Rowland Phototypesetting Limited, Bury St Edmunds, Suffolk
and printed by St Edmundsbury Press
Bury St Edmunds, Suffolk
Bound by Weatherby Woolnough

Contents

List of illustrations

35   Readily available louvered doors in slides.
36   A thin strip of 3/16″ ply used for the surround.
37   Cupboard doors and apertures look neat when the end grain of the ply is covered with teak or mahogany trim.
38   Unbreakable glass in main companion-way admits more light.
39   Useful bedside cupboards and shelves.
40 & 41   A useful size of chart table, raised and lowered.
42   Chart table with secure seating for navigator.
43   Main companion-way steps bracketed and bolted for security.
44   Handholds help on long steps.
45   Internal handhold bolted through to external one.
46   Upright tubular pillars make good handholds as well as bracing up half bulkheads and coachroofs.
47   Plugs from a piece of scrap timber give a much better finish than filler for screw holes.
48   Extractor vent built into roof liner battens.
49   Where carpet might block off air circulation, a vent in the door will replace it, and is sound policy anyway.
50   A comprehensive engine and sterngear kit.
51   Good engine access. View from forward through hatch in main bulkhead beneath companion-way steps.
52   Bukh 36-hp diesel with gear-box.
53   Bukh 36-hp diesel with sail drive.
54   Bukh 10-hp diesel.
55   Bukh 20-hp diesel.
56   GKN Aquadrive.
57   Propshaft bracket containing cutlass bearing and propeller. Single engine installation on centreline.
58   A selection of marine quality lights.
59   Wiring loom from Peter Smailes Circuit Marine.
60   Through-deck watertight glands and outside light.
61 & 62   Easily accessible switch panel with cupboard space behind.
63 & 64   Toilet, shower, cupboards, work top and sink all in 4′ square.
65   GRP tanks forming an integral part of a hull.
66   Tank construction.
67   Keel to coachroof pillar supporting hardwood mast pad.
68   Rear of engine. 'A' frame fabrication in mild steel sits on engine bearers and supports mizzen mast.
69 & 70   Space is found for a heater; handhold pillars also stop the hot flue being grabbed.
71, 72 & 73   Battens to achieve a smooth lining self-tapped into a distorted steel bulkhead.

Picture credits

Sadler Yachts: 1, 2, 15, 50; Jenny Saunders: 3, 4, 5, 6, 7, 8, 9, 12A; Strand Glassfibre: 10, 11, 12, 13, 14, 16, 17; Tyler Mouldings: 18, 19, 20, 65, 66; David Everett: 21–49, 51, 57–64, 67–73; South Western Marine Factors: 52–55; Halyard Marine: 56.

Acknowledgements

The author would like to thank the following for technical advice and help: Peter Smailes of Peter Smailes Circuit Marine; David Hobbis of Tyler Mouldings; and Brian Lacey, builder of *Renascent*, shown in many of the photographs. For sending information and photographs: South Western Marine Factors; Sadler Yachts Ltd; Halyard Marine; Strand Glassfibre; Golden Arrow Marine Ltd; Calor Gas Ltd; I.T.T. Fluid Handling Ltd; and Barton Abrasives Ltd. And lastly, for supplying some excellent photographs, Jenny and Terry Saunders.

To Ann

Preface

Completing your own boat from a basic shell can be a very rewarding and satisfying task. It can be therapeutic, bringing out talents you never knew you had. It can introduce you to a new circle of friends who are fellow enthusiasts. It can also be the only way that some of us can afford to end up with the kind of boat that would otherwise remain a dream.

Some dreams reach launching day, others founder on the way, sometimes predictably, sometimes through bad luck. To ensure success, it seems, the single most important factor is to be realistic about the whole scheme. The task on which you are about to embark is not easy. Absorbing? Yes. Creative? Certainly, but no doddle.

Basically, what you are going to save in cost over the ready-to-sail, fully-in-commission boat is the labour (plus iniquitous VAT on the same). This is the commodity you are going to supply, in considerable quantities, mostly during those hours that others call leisure time, for an indefinite period that usually turns out to be at least twice as long as you anticipated.

Your new circle of friends soon become necessary. At least they think the same way as you, and have the same problems. A lot of your old ones, having at first considered you an interesting eccentric, will reach the eventual conclusion that you have become unsociable, crazy, or both, and will start to seek more stable and respectable company to meet at all the parties you now never seem to have time to attend. No bad thing either, because once committed to the boat you probably won't have any spare cash for socializing anyway!

Are you off the idea yet? How about your partner? The latter is a very pertinent point. If there are two of you involved enthusiasm must be a joint thing, otherwise you are heading for disaster. A divorce could cost the price of a new mast, or hold up the supply of plywood for the bulkheads! This could be quite a set-back to the building programme, and think of all the haggling over who owns the echosounder, the ten-gallon drum of resin etc. It has been known to happen!

At least part of my intention in this book is to see that it doesn't happen to you. It may, of course, be that this is not your first project, and so you know most of the pitfalls, in which case, bear with me a little while. There are other optimistic sailors who are about to leap in feet first, and will need a little guidance.

It is true of at least two failed projects I know of that a little more forethought would have made them successful. Most of us are optimists at heart, and this is a very useful state of mind provided it is tempered with realism. It is very easy to see a hull advertised in a magazine and imagine yourself halfway to the West Indies, a dazzling sun high-lighting white wavelets against the deep blue sea, dolphins playfully leaping around you, and flying fish desperately trying to escape the denizens of the deep. You know the sort of thing? Well before you get there, there is just this little matter of fitting out, which may be troublesome for those impatient to get to sea, but it has to be done.

During the course of completion you will find jobs that are easy, hard, interesting, tedious, demanding, smelly, dirty and so on, but when it is all over you will be able to enjoy that feeling of smug satisfaction that you did it all yourself, and have the callouses and scars to prove it.

1 · Choosing and buying

Among those readers who are rash enough to consider completing their own hull, despite my warnings, there may be many who have had little or nothing to do with boats before. Don't let this put you off. It is, after all, very sensible to want a boat. The thing is, what sort of boat to buy?

To answer this question you will need to know roughly what you want to do, which may sound obvious, but maybe you haven't yet had the chance to find out, or the time.

Boats have a magnetic fascination wherever you float them. The potential world girdler may be a far cry from the canal-cruising devotee, but both will no doubt enjoy their pastime with equal fervour.

A glance through the charter and holiday sections in the yachting Press will show you just how many opportunities there are of gaining experience in all aspects of boating, and this can be a key factor in the success of your project. There is not much point in spending your valuable time, effort and money on an ocean-cruising yacht only to find that you are incurably seasick, any more than to fit out a canal cruiser and discover that inland waterways restrict you and make you long for the open sea for which your boat is totally unsuitable.

A cheaper way to gain experience is to advertise your services as crew, or to nose around marinas and chat to people. A few well chosen compliments to an owner will often work wonders. I went across the Channel to Fécamp a short while back, with a friend who was heading south. There were two of us to come back, and it was either the bus to Dieppe and the ferry, or hitch a lift. On the jetty next to us there was a boat marked 'Newhaven' obviously preparing to leave, so we simply asked for a lift, offered to help, and nineteen hours later we were back in Brighton. It can't hurt to ask, they can only say no. If you are accepted, be honest about your experience or lack of, show willing and you may get some free tuition.

Whichever method you choose, experience is the only thing to help you decide on the right kind of boat, and the sort of cruising you find most satisfying.

The next thing is to have a very good notion of the amount of money you can afford.

This is where you must be brutally honest with yourself. Running out of money probably accounts for a good fifty per cent of failures, and don't kid yourself that you will recover what you have spent by selling a part-completed hull. You won't! People looking for such a hull know that the owner will probably accept a fraction of its true value just to get free from an embarrassing situation.

Don't aim too high, it is much better to be able to sail in a boat that may lack the ultimate in comfort than to end up with a potential luxury yacht you can never afford to finish. Apart from the frustration of realizing that you have bitten off more than you can chew, this sort of bitter disillusionment could well poison your attitude towards boats altogether, which would be a shame, when a more modest beginning could have resulted in years of enjoyment.

It is important to remember that it will cost more than you think anyway. Inflation sees to that. So if you plan for a realistic budget, the project may take longer, but at least you have a chance of winning.

The price of fitting out a hull rises quite incredibly with the increase of overall beam and length. A forty-footer, for example, may well work out four or five times as much as a twenty-footer. There is a very good reason for this: everything will have to be bigger—masts, sails, engine or engines, anchors, winches etc. Apart from this, a lot more of every building material will be used, and many things will have to be of a heavier gauge and stronger. A look at the price of completed boats will give you some idea of cost in proportion to size.

Although the empty hull and superstructure may look as though it is almost ready to sail away, it is far from it. For a basic guide, however economically you manage to build your boat, it will probably cost more than half the manufacturer's price rigged and ready to sail, and this is assuming you are able to marinize a second-hand road-going engine and make up a lot of your own equipment. If you intend to buy every item of equipment brand new, from marine suppliers, then two-thirds will probably be nearer the mark.

It is impossible to say exactly what it is going to cost you. It depends too much on the way you set about it. Some builders are only happy if they buy the best, and others are satisfied with less. By this I don't mean sub-standard or potentially weak and dangerous things, but there is a great deal of difference in the price of stainless steel fittings as against galvanized iron; of Perspex ports or windows against aluminium-framed sliding or opening windows etc. A lot of it is a matter of choice. A cosmetic teak-laid deck looks terrific, but you can get by without it.

The other major factor governing your budget is the amount of time over which you intend to spread it. I have just read of one gentleman who has already taken eight years to part-complete his seventy-foot catamaran, and reckons another eight years should see it finished! Most of us are not that patient.

Another factor in the battle to succeed is not to have a project that stretches so far away into the future that you become bored with it. Taking around thirty feet as a popular size of vessel, and assuming in this case you start with a hull and superstructure, and work evenings, weekends and holidays, between two and three years would seem to be a reasonable expectation of building time. Single-handed, that is. Some builders of my acquaintance are quicker, and then again I have known some take five or six years.

Admittedly the longer you take the more you come under the grip of inflation, but on the other side of the coin, the completed boat will be worth more for the same reason. At least this way, your gear can be bought as you need it. It all depends how impatient you are to begin sailing.

Keeping, for the moment, to boats around thirty feet, the most expensive item after the purchase of the hull will be the engine, gear-box and sterngear package. In a twin-screw motor cruiser, this installation may well cost even more than the hull.

In these days of increased competition, a lot of manufacturers are offering complete package deals at very reasonable prices, so it pays to shop around.

Second-hand goods should not necessarily be spurned. There are many reasons why a hopeful builder may not be able to complete the job, and the products of such tragedies sometimes appear on the market at very moderate prices, so it is wise to keep a beady eye on the small ads. In this instance, a lot of items may well be new and unused, although deterioration could have been caused by time, so use caution, or better still, expert advice.

Although you are protected to some extent by the Sale of Goods Act, and the Trades Description Act etc., the person from whom you are buying may be broke, so your claim in the case of faulty goods is unlikely to be of much benefit.

If you intend buying a complete hull and superstructure second-hand, whether GRP, steel or ferro-cement etc., it is advisable to enlist the services of a qualified surveyor, even though it may appear sound. Nine times out of ten you could get a real bargain, but the tenth could have all sorts of faults built into it that are not apparent to the amateur, and the vendor is not necessarily going to be nice enough to tell you all about it, even presuming he knows.

A glance through most yachting magazines will reveal plenty of manufacturers of hulls and superstructures in various stages of completion, to suit all pockets, and this brings in another possible factor. It may well be that time is your problem rather than money, and that you want something you can complete in a fortnight's holiday and a few weekends.

Most manufacturers will be only too willing to advise you, provided you can tell them how much you want to spend. They will also help in the question of finance, and the more progressive ones can even offer DIY boatyard facilities in certain areas where you can finish off your own boat under their expert guidance. Some also hire tools, have the necessary materials for sale, and qualified labour to help you over the difficult hurdles.

Naturally these services don't come free, not all of them anyway, but if you are unsure of your ability then this way of approaching the problem could be very useful, and go a long way to ensuring that you end up with a safe, seaworthy craft.

The stages at which you can buy most types of boat are usually offered as follows:

a Hull only
b Hull and deck
c Hull, deck and superstructure
d As above, but bonded together
e As above, plus ballast fitted and encapsulated
f As above, plus main bulkheads supplied
g As above, plus main bulkheads fitted
h As above, plus all bulkheads fitted
i As above, plus various internal mouldings
j As above, plus engine beds fitted
k As above, plus engine, stern tube and propshaft fitted

And so on, with maybe engine fitted and working, all internal wiring done, fuel tanks fitted and plumbed etc. So depending on your purse, or time available, it is possible to start right at the beginning or quite near the end.

These alternatives might also suit those who feel that the carpentry side of the scheme can be coped with, but not the mechanics. This being the case, it can often work out cheaper to have the manufacturer do the engine installation than to call in a professional later on. This is because the manufacturer, especially those also selling completed boats, will have all the jigs, looms and equipment to hand, plus a fitter who has done it all many times before, whereas the newcomer will have to start from scratch.

The manufacturer will also get a discount on engines and equip-

1:   Internal mouldings in GRP

2:   Hull and deck with main bulkheads and mouldings fitted

ment, and, as a sales inducement, may make various package offers which are very attractive.

Although the list of completion stages is only a general guide, as some builders will only sell the basic hull, while others will do all the above and more if asked, it obviously pays to explore the market thoroughly and do a lot of soul-searching regarding capability, budget and help that may be available to you before making your choice.

Of course, with enough time, patience and determination at your disposal, you will probably find it possible to do everything yourself. Indeed, you may be in that financial position (and you're not alone mate!) that makes the above course essential. This, only you can decide. There are short-cuts for those who want them and are prepared to pay for the privilege.

There will, of course, be those gifted, ambitious and brave souls who want to start right at the beginning, with a set of drawings and a lot of hope, but although this is naturally the cheapest way to get a boat together it comes outside the scope of this book, at least until the fitting out stage is reached.

Capability is a somewhat nebulous factor. Many people who fit out their own hulls have never turned their hand to anything practical in their lives before. Some discover an aptitude previously unrealized, while most others become proficient in the course of learning by their initial mistakes and asking a lot of questions.

Confidence in your ability to succeed is a great asset, and helps you to ignore all those who seem to take great delight in telling you how you will inevitably come unstuck for one reason or another. Don't be too hard on these doubters, they are probably frustrated boat builders who lack the nerve to have a go themselves.

If your intention is to start off with a hull, deck and superstructure, all bonded together, which is probably the most popular course, then provided care is taken to put the main bulkheads where they are needed for strength, for mast support etc., the basic boat can be fairly seaworthy even if the rest of the interior joinery is not first-rate. The boat can be used and enjoyed, and it is really only when and if it comes to be sold that the effect of a poor finish will be felt—in the price!

Although some potentially dangerous lash-ups are launched, a surprising amount of DIY boats end up quite adequately sound, even if a few might lack polish. I believe this is because few people approach this sort of project casually. It is neither a small undertaking nor a trifling investment, and most amateur builders I have met very much want to end up with a boat of which they can be proud. In pursuit of this aim, they make sure to glean the necessary information and knowledge from one source or another, seeking qualified help if it becomes essential.

Starting out with a hull only will certainly cut down the initial outlay, but before deciding on this course, the unskilled builder should consider a few factors.

Whereas the hull, deck and superstructure, pre-bonded, will normally be rigid enough to maintain the shape of the boat, the hull only is often quite flexible. Although most manufacturers will glass in, or, in the case of steel hulls, tack weld temporary support beams to retain the shape, far more care and expertise is needed to build in integral strength.

A complete shell often makes it possible to work inside regardless of weather conditions, but with hull only, some sort of temporary shelter is a must.

It may well be that you prefer a wooden superstructure, and there is no doubt that if well constructed, it can look far superior to most other materials. Conversely though, if poorly made, it can look a lot worse.

Most people I have spoken to who started from a hull only and no previous experience were surprised how long the deck, coamings and coachroof took to build, and how difficult it was to make them strong and watertight. Although the sense of achievement and pride seemed to be greater in the finished craft, at least half reckoned that if they ever built another boat they would start with a complete shell, and begin sailing a lot quicker.

This is clearly a matter of individual choice, but one that needs careful consideration. If you feel that nothing but wood will do for you, and the extra time the job will take is acceptable, then no more need be said, but don't be lured by the fact that it may work out cheaper without weighing up the pros and cons.

If you are inexperienced with carpentry but would still like a wooden superstructure, a good method of getting your hand in is to build a marine ply dinghy. This has the dual advantage of proving to yourself whether, at this stage, you have the aptitude, and also providing you with a tender for future use. Or, of course, you can sell the dinghy to help finance the boat.

The building of a good, watertight dinghy can be a very exacting job; you will also find out how much you enjoy doing this sort of thing, without laying out a great deal of money. Better an incomplete dinghy on your hands than a thirty-foot cruiser!

Once more, reference to the 'kits' section of the yachting Press will produce the necessary information on suppliers.

Attempting a small pram dinghy, which will take no more than a few evenings and a couple of weekends in your garage—or front room for that matter (make sure it will pass through the door or window!), will no doubt help you if you are wavering in your decision whether or not to start off with a complete shell. There is just one other way of approaching the problem. If the exercise was more or less successful, and you felt you would quickly improve with more practice, there is no reason why you shouldn't leave the deck and superstructure until the interior is complete, provided you can work under cover. Many manufacturers build up glass fibre boats this way because it is easier to fit bulkheads from the top than to struggle through narrow entrances with them. In fact, this way they can often go in in one piece instead of having to divide them up for access reasons. It is most important in this case, though, that your building shelter is a good one. It would be a pity to have a near complete interior ruined by becoming water-logged.

With so many choices available, don't be afraid to ask the manufacturer for all the advice you need, and be frank about how much you can afford and how much knowledge you possess with regard to building. They will usually give you all the help possible, whether practical advice, or in arranging finance, delivery, insurance etc. Time and competition has fortunately weeded out most of the cowboys, and the firms that still exist are generally sound, informative and knowledgeable. In most cases, and this can be really useful to you, they are quite willing for you to go and have a nosey at the completed article, to see how various things are done, and as you will probably find, if you are like me, that after a week or so you have forgotten a lot of vital factors, a phone call will usually get you in for another look.

Seeing the boat in various stages of construction can also be extremely useful, but for the yard's sake, do make sure it is convenient. A little consideration on your part will usually ensure your welcome on future occasions.

My final word on choosing the type of craft you want is to bear in mind that the perfect boat doesn't exist, but careful selection can produce a pretty good compromise. For instance, if you feel you want to go canal cruising, but also fancy going out to sea sometimes, there are estuary cruisers that will do both, although this may mean that you are barred from the very narrow canals.

If coastal cruising takes your fancy, and you like nosing up shallow inlets, then a shallow draft, possibly twin bilge-keel or centre-board yacht will be more suitable than the deep keel 'blue water' type.

Read magazines, talk to people and manufacturers, and with the vast selection available you are bound to find one that comes near to suiting your requirements. If you decide after a season or two that you need a boat to perform a different use, you can always sell it and buy another. At least the experience you have gained will give you a much better idea of what you want next time.

Having made your choice on the type of boat you want, the next consideration is the type of material it is to be made from. To some extent this may be governed by the use. For example, a canal barge that is certain to take at least some regular punishment, however well handled, by squeezing through narrow locks etc., is best made from

steel and painted black so it doesn't show up oil stains, marks from
rubber tyre fenders and so on. True, a lot of very good canal cruisers
are made from GRP, but unless great care is taken they can show their
age quite quickly, and spoil the skipper's peace of mind during tight
manoeuvring.

For most other uses the material is more a matter of choice or
convenience, or maybe price.

For quite a few years now, GRP (glass reinforced plastic), otherwise
called resinglass or fibreglass, has enjoyed a large share of the popular
boat market—a trend that looks like continuing for a while yet.

In the early days, GRP really looked like being the answer to the
would-be boat manufacturer's prayer. For years, in fact centuries,
boat building had been the province of highly skilled craftsmen.
Suddenly, for the initial investment of a mould, boat shells could be
turned out like hot cakes with virtually unskilled labour. What was
more, the resulting product, if made under the right conditions, was
strong, impervious to weathering, watertight and relatively easy to
maintain.

Social and economic conditions were just right for this sort of
breakthrough, and the industry boomed. GRP became big business.
Within a very short while it was difficult to find a wooden boat at the
Boat Show. The skill of the traditional boat-builder joined the ranks of
the dying trades.

Together with the major firms, many of whom are still in the
forefront due to wise investment in research and improvement, the
'get rich quick' atmosphere inevitably attracted the cowboy element
who took little notice of building conditions and turned out hulls
without proper control of temperature or humidity, with scant attention to the laying-up process, and often with inferior or padded-out
resins.

Consequently, together with the really good boats, some really
dreadful rubbish came on the market, and a lot of unlucky owners
found themselves with boats that dulled or looked shoddy very
quickly because of poor quality or thin gel coats, delamination
problems caused by the capillary action of water seeping into bad
lay-ups and any number of other evils which proved that GRP, like
any other material, has to be handled competently.

In the main, GRP shells from a reputable manufacturer are as
suitable as any other material, and more convenient than some.

Unfortunately, being an oil-based product, prices are rising rapid-
ly, and although this has allowed some other materials to gain their
rightful share of the market, it is likely that GRP will retain the lion's
share because of its other advantages. Not the least of these is that
adding bulkheads and other structures needs care rather than skill.
There is no reason why the newcomer to GRP, provided simple

instructions are followed, shouldn't achieve rapid if not instant success.

Also, for the builder who wants to start sailing quickly, many manufacturers provide additional mouldings for galleys, dinettes, benches, shower compartments, self-draining cockpits and so on. Admittedly it isn't everyone's choice to be surrounded by plastic, but it does cut down the amount of carpentry necessary, and must speed up the project.

Contrary to early thinking GRP is not completely perfect. Maintenance is less than most other materials, but it still needs to be done. Barnacles and weed get an amazing grip on it if not antifouled regularly, and the more virile of the former seem quite capable of taking lumps of gelcoat with them when scraped off. The topsides also need cleaning and polishing often if a smart appearance is to be retained.

Another factor often gloated over by owners of steel and ferrocement boats is the fire risk inherent in GRP. Although thankfully rare, fire at sea must be a horrifying experience, and stringent precautions must be taken to avoid it. With an engine and a galley, it is impossible not to carry inflammable fuel on board, let alone timber, plastic linings, foam rubber, insulation material etc. So although GRP is at greater risk, being itself very inflammable, any boat can be a floating death-trap if safety has been neglected at the installation stage. There are plenty of petrol-powered GRP boats around which have survived happily for years on care, common sense and normal safety precautions.

Fires very seldom just 'happen', and even GRP is not that easy to ignite, so if a careless smoker sets the bed alight, the blaze can usually be brought under control in time with the right equipment and prompt action, or the burning bedding (and smoker) can be thrown overboard.

A fire blanket in the galley, strategically placed extinguishers and a gas alarm should be adequate for all situations except explosions, and with safe installations and regular maintenance the latter shouldn't happen.

So don't let talk of fire risk put you off GRP. If the risk was unreasonable, insurance companies wouldn't have provided cover all this time.

Helped a great deal by the reawakening of interest in canal and river cruising, the availability of steel hulls for home completion has enjoyed a boom in recent years. Also, the price of a steel hull is now very much in line with GRP.

The most popular steel hulls for inland cruising are variations of the traditional narrow boat, which, with its beam of only 6' 10", is narrow enough to negotiate all the locks of the UK canal system, some of which are only seven feet in width. The original narrow boats were some seventy feet in length, and many of today's versions are the same, but they are usually sold by the foot, and so it is possible to have one anywhere between twenty and seventy feet depending on the use, the number of berths required and the price you want to pay.

Since a large part of the canal system is navigable by wider boats, beamier versions are now being produced to give better internal accommodation.

I mention this particular type of boat separately because it is so different from other kinds of boat you are likely to be fitting out. Apart from a canoe-like bow and a rounded stern, the rest of the length is flat-bottomed and straight-sided. This is why they can be sold by the foot, literally just adding to the midship section to achieve the desired length.

Another important point is the ease of fitting out. The rounded stern carries the engine, and the bow section is usually used for stowage. This means that the internal area is all straight lines. Bearing in mind that one of the main difficulties of building accommodation into a conventional boat is trying to achieve squares and levels where every part of the hull and superstructure curves in different directions, the narrow boat must be the simplest of all to complete.

Apart from narrow boats, and their broader cousins, barges, steel has, until recently, been more the domain of the commercial ship and large motor yacht than of small pleasure craft, except in Holland where a lack of timber engendered a thriving steel yacht building industry years ago.

Like GRP a steel hull does not need the services of a traditional boat-builder, only a competent welder and fabricator. Controlled conditions are necessary only for the comfort of the welders, and the finished result is a very strong, watertight shell which with reasonable maintenance will give as long a life as any other type of material that is looked after.

Apart from the greatly reduced fire risk—and this is a valid point, because a fire can often be contained and dealt with in the compartment where it started, and even a really bad fire will often leave a gutted but re-usable hull—one of the main advantages of steel, from a safety viewpoint, is that a collision with heavy driftwood tends to result in a dent rather than a hole.

As a steel shell of a pleasure-sized yacht is normally rigid without bulkheads, the latter have to be added more for the purpose of dividing the boat into the desired compartments than to build in strength. It is usually quite sufficient to bolt them on to the frames or lugs provided which can simplify the fitting out process.

Without elaborate rolling equipment, it is difficult to bend steel in more than one direction, so apart from the very expensive steel hulls, the majority will be hard-chine or multi-chine designs, i.e. there will be 'corners' rather than curves on a line taken from the deck to the keel, much the same as when Marine ply was used widely, and for the same reason.

As, in a good design, the chine is below the water-line for most if not all of its length, this factor doesn't make much difference outside personal preference. Aesthetically, a sweetly curved hull may be preferable, but for sailing performance there is not much to choose between the two.

Corrosion can be a problem, as steel is prone to rusting, and a mixture of dissimilar metals below the water-line, especially in salt water, can promote galvanic action, but this also can be controlled effectively as will be explained in a later chapter.

Other advantages of steel are ease and comparative cheapness to repair, and the fact that a lot of deck fittings which normally require through bolting can simply be welded on. Some if not all of these will or can be supplied with the hull, which again cuts out work later on and shortens the building programme.

If you decide on steel, obviously the ability to weld is an advantage and a saving. Small, portable electric welding sets are not expensive when compared to the price of most power tools, and most welders will tell you that the technique for the sort of simple jobs you will want to do can be picked up in half an hour of instruction. Indeed, some steel boat owners I have spoken to are entirely self-taught, apart from having read up on the subject.

Reading a book like *Own a Steel Boat* by Mike Pratt (Hollis & Carter Ltd) will soon soothe any fears you may have on running or working on a boat of this material.

Ferro-cement hulls for home completion are also a fairly recent development. Traditionally the builder has started from scratch and done the whole job, but adverts in the yachting Press show an increasing number of firms selling hulls, decks and superstructures.

Contrary to my own belief, not so very many years ago, that a hull made from this material would shatter into a million fragments under the smallest of impacts, the ferro boat has proved to be extremely strong, and by now, well proven by ocean sailing and commercial work.

The principle of steel reinforced cement or concrete is not new. However, as such structures are normally fairly colossal, it must have taken a very inventive mind to picture it as a suitable boat-building material. Despite the obvious hurdles of weight and thickness, development since the war has overcome the snags and provided the means of building good boats fairly economically.

The building of the armature or basket, and the plastering of the same comes outside the scope of this book on ready-made shells, but anyone interested in finding out how it is done would be well advised to read *The First Ferro Boat Book* by Pete Greenfield (Hollis & Carter Ltd), which is both informative and entertaining and based largely on personal experience.

The fact that ferro-cement boats have taken a while to become accepted more widely is no doubt partly due to the fact that some of the early examples were very poorly finished, to put it kindly. Over the years though, techniques have become refined until it is now difficult to tell a good example from a GRP hull.

As the finished product is on the heavy side, the hulls made for home completion are mostly 'blue water' types, with a deep draught and traditional heavy displacement lines. Unlike GRP or steel, there is a limit to how thin, and therefore light, the hull can be made, so with rare exceptions the material is mostly used for boats of thirty feet and upwards where weight is not a limiting factor.

A great deal of care is necessary in the building and especially the curing of a ferro hull, so if you are buying from an amateur builder, just as with steel, a surveyor specializing in the material could save you a lot of future problems.

An example of a major problem encountered by some unfortunate buyers is finding that all the necessary apertures for ports, scuppers, and skin fittings are not catered for. Whereas steel and GRP can both be cut with normal power tools, ferro-cement not only needs very sophisticated cutting equipment, but the act of cutting can weaken the structure as well as exposing steel which can then rust up inside the cement eventually causing more weakness.

Like its counterparts, ferro-cement will need the usual amount of upkeep—probably as much as GRP, and marginally less than steel.

As this book is mainly about the fitting out of ready-made hulls and superstructures, as offered for home completion by numerous manu-facturers, GRP, steel and ferro-cement, in order of present popular-ity, cover the range of what is currently available. Other types, such as GRP foam sandwich, hot or cold moulded mahogany, marine ply, timber or aluminium may become available from time to time from either an amateur builder who is unable to finish the job, or a manufacturer who is either going out of business, or switching to a different material. Indeed some yards may supply you with a hull if you ask them, although it is not their normal practice.

Although all cruising sized boats need accommodation of some sort built into them, some, which are designed to be very lightweight, multihulls for example, also need very light furniture and fittings. A catamaran or trimaran to which too much weight is added can become lethal. It is most important, if buying a specialized type of boat or a 'one off', to arm yourself with the necessary information, preferably from the designer, or a builder who is familiar with the type.

2 · All those vital preparations

Having decided what type of hull to fit out, the next major consideration will be where to build it, and here, the size of the hull is quite relevant.

Of course, if you have a farm, or smallholding, or even a large garden, the problem may be non-existent. I say 'may' because large gardens tend to be in nice neighbourhoods, which don't necessarily abound with nice neighbours. Yours may be a spoil-sport, and object to his outlook being blotted out by a large hull, wood shavings blowing all over his lawn, noise pollution from your power tools, and the fact that from the deck you can now see his wife sunbathing in the nude.

You can't please everyone, of course, but you can forestall a lot of aggravation by finding out in advance if anyone is likely to object, including the local council.

Most sailing boats of around thirty feet are at least eight feet from the top of the superstructure to the keel. If you intend working under a temporary cover, with some sort of headroom on deck, you are talking in terms of fourteen or fifteen feet, which could be an eyesore for even the best of neighbours. There could be alternative positions which would cause less annoyance. Talking about it usually helps.

Building in your own garden must be best, if it is feasible, for a number of reasons. It is free; power and water are on hand, and maybe a garage for storing materials once the car is relegated to the driveway; and overall security is better. Make sure the crane has access, though. A representative from the crane firm can tell you.

If the crane has to go off the road, it may be necessary to shore up the pavement with railway sleepers or something similar. The crane company will be able to advise you here, but if the manoeuvre is likely to endanger water or gas mains get advice from those two authorities as well. They are usually very helpful, and damage to public services can be expensive.

A word about cranes. The nearer the crane can get to the boat the smaller it need be; large cranes are very expensive. A friend of mine built a thirty-five-foot trimaran in his back garden, this being the only possibility, and six years later it had to be winched right over the house by a twenty-five ton crane with an extended jib, even though the boat weighed under two tons. So build where the crane can get close if possible.

With smaller boats craning might be avoided altogether by building a scaffolding gantry where the trailer the boat is delivered on can be backed right underneath, the boat hoisted up a few inches on slings so the trailer can be towed clear, and then the boat lowered onto its level bed. The gantry can then be covered to form a temporary shed. Before adopting this course, however, check very carefully the weight the lifting points will take, and also the block and tackles.

Another alternative is to jack up the bow a few inches using a hydraulic bottle jack and softwood pad, until a beam of around 8″ × 6″ (or planks on edge bolted together) can be slid under the bilge-keels, and supported on blocks wider than the trailer's overall width. The same process is then carried out under the skeg, and the trailer can be withdrawn and extra support placed as necessary.

For a lot of builders, the garden, assuming there is one, will not be adequate and an alternative spot will have to be found. Such spots can be very difficult to find, especially one where power can be supplied, and without power, the project will take much longer and in some cases it will be impossible.

For many reasons, a secluded corner of a boatyard is a good place, because they will be aware of your needs and most likely able to supply advice and possibly even tools. Some yards, as mentioned in the last chapter, are specially equipped for DIY builders, and these usually advertise in the yachting Press. Some yacht clubs also have areas where members can fit out their boats.

A good deal of hunting around may be necessary, but when you find somewhere, especially if it is on private land, make sure you have the blessing of the right authority. Being asked to move before the boat is complete could prove a crippling expense. Keep it as local as possible—it is expensive and time-consuming to keep travelling a long way to and fro—and make sure power, water if possible and preferably toilet facilities are on hand. Check that a crane can get to it without undue trouble (time means money here), and lastly that the site is moderately level.

Before delivery, it is desirable to make a level bed on which the boat can stand. Beds I have seen vary a lot, from the construction of a level concrete platform and a building cradle with access stairs at the top end, right down to the way I did it with my first effort at fitting out, at the very bottom end.

This was a thirty-one-foot motor boat shell with twin keels to help it

3–9: Launching sequence of *Renascent*. Note webbing strops. In this case spreaders were considered unnecessary, but the lifelines have been slackened to avoid bending stanchions

stand level on the mud, which was where it was put, on a tidal mud berth. I even got by without a crane, because the driver of the low loader that delivered it reckoned he could back his trailer down a public hard until the boat could be floated off. With some levering and shoving this was accomplished, with what cost to his trailer I never did find out, being, as it was, submerged right up to the cab in salt water.

Although this course of action was necessary for me at the time, because as soon as it floated off the trailer the boat became my home for some three years, it is not one I would recommend. Apart from it being almost impossible to achieve a really true level or vertical, it is not easy to live in a boat you are building. Conditions were somewhat primitive at first. The only advantage I can think of is that skin fittings had to be fitted in between tides, and this way it quickly became apparent if they leaked. Better than finding out just after a crane lowers you into a deep-water mooring, because in this case you either have to use more crane time to fix the trouble, or find somewhere to beach the boat.

The very least you should have for a level bed are two or three (more with a long keel) railway sleepers, or oak fence posts levelled out on a surface that won't subside as soon as the shell is lowered on to it.

A boat with strong twin bilge-keels will stand up without assistance, although the bilge-keels will not be quite as deep as the main keel (if there is one) and will need extra chocks under them. Slim wooden wedges are useful here, both to harden up the chocks and for side-to-side adjustment.

If you are likely to be on a tidal berth eventually, and will therefore take the ground regularly, it will be advisable to have timber reinforcement under the bilge-keels to protect the gelcoat. Some manufacturers fit these as an optional extra, and paying a little more at this stage will obviate having to jack up the hull later.

On many modern hulls aimed at the DIY market, the main keel is parallel to the water-line, and those with two bilge-keels and a skeg are also often made to sit level provided they are on a level surface. Only the drawings can tell you, so you will need access to these before delivery. The main factor is that the water-line is level, because it is on this line that the boat is designed to float, so if it is levelled up fore and aft and athwart before you start building, a plumb-line will ensure that all the bulkheads go in vertical and that all the doorways are upright. Likewise, a spirit-level will get all the horizontal surfaces right, and both vertical and horizontal surfaces will still be right when you are afloat.

In the case of deep-keeled boats, a building cradle is favourite. Many people do use chocks and wedges, but it is possible to knock these out of place by accident, and they are far more difficult to level up.

When you wander around boatyards and see plenty of deep-keel yachts supported solely by chocks and wedges, the system may seem perfectly adequate, but in fact, most of these boats will only be out of the water for bottom painting or minor repairs. Fitting out is a bit different because one or more people will be spending a lot of time walking around inside, heaving heavy sheets of ply around and constantly transferring weight from one point to another.

I personally would not recommend this method. Even if the chocks remained firm throughout, they could well cause distortion to an empty shell, and result in stress points when removed. For the same reason, mooring legs should not be used until sufficient internal support has been added.

Before deciding against the extra expense of a cradle, check with the manufacturer. In the majority of cases they will advise you to use one. Some yards will supply a cradle with the boat at a reasonable charge, and others will hire you one for the duration of building. Either course will probably be as cheap as building your own, and it is bound to be the right design for the boat. It will then be up to you merely to provide level, firm ground on which to site it.

If you have to build one, don't be mean with the timber, or the bolts which hold it together. Soft wood or even demolition timber, provided it is sound, is quite adequate. The design will depend on the shape and length of the keel, and skeg if there is a separate one. Most manufacturers will provide a drawing at least, and as this will apply to the particular type of boat, it should be followed carefully, and made in plenty of time before delivery.

Access stairs are popular with some people, and they are certainly more convenient for carrying heavy loads up into the boat than a ladder. There are two schools of thought on this one though, as they also provide access for anyone anytime. For this reason many builders put up with a ladder or steps which can be removed completely or padlocked to the cradle in such a way that they cannot be used to get aboard.

Being quite high off the ground it is surprisingly difficult to climb on to the deck of a boat without some sort of assistance, as you will no doubt find out the first time you forget to bring the steps. This at least makes the boat secure from casual snoopers in your absence.

A quick revision for pre-delivery preparations: if the hull has twin keels and a skeg, have baulks of timber and wedges handy, the latter for firming up and adjusting slight discrepancies in the level. If a cradle is being used, the ground under it needs to be completely level. It is much easier to do this before the weight of the boat is added, and wedging up one corner of the cradle could cause distortion.

Finally, make sure you have arranged building cover insurance with a good company, and check that either this, or the delivery firm's own insurance, includes the delivery journey.

The manufacturer will often be pleased to arrange the delivery details for you, and in this case the driver will probably be well used to transporting the particular shape of boat, and be tooled up for it. If you live well outside their area they may leave it to you to organize a crane, should it be necessary.

If you are buying privately it will probably be necessary for you to arrange both, unless the delivery firm is local and makes use of the same crane-hire company all the time.

If it is left to you, timing is very important. It could be costly if the lorry is held up, and the crane kept waiting for a couple of hours. Some firms hire their cranes on an hourly basis, and some make a minimum charge for a set period and then charge by each additional hour. Time is normally charged from the time they leave their depot until the time they return, which is why a local firm is the best to use. Also, crane firms rarely accept responsibility for any accidental damage that may occur during the operation, which is why your insurance must be in order.

Should you be doing your building at a boatyard, it is more than likely that cranes will make fairly frequent visits during spring and autumn as a lot of owners have their boats lifted out at the end of the season for annual maintenance, and put back at the beginning of the next season. If you can therefore arrange your delivery at one of these times, a great saving can be made by sharing the charges with a few other boats.

When your boat finally arrives, don't be afraid to ask advice from the driver or the crane operator if there is anything about which you are unsure. The chances are they have both moved boats many times before, and they are normally very good at it, with few exceptions. If you are unlucky enough to be sent a novice, or an unfeeling operator who is in a hurry to get home for lunch, there are a few points to bear in mind. Firstly, make sure the crane is provided with slings. These are flat webbing strops about six or eight inches wide and long enough to go under the keel and still clear each side deck by a couple of feet. Chains must only be used from the loop at each end of the slings up to the lifting hook. On no account allow the operator to lift the boat on chains, which can cause considerable surface damage.

Spreaders of a similar size to scaffold planks should be laid across the deck from one side to the other of each sling. These should be a few inches greater than the beam of the boat, and will stop any crushing effect as the boat is lifted. The operator should also use chains as long as possible as this also helps to reduce the inward pull.

Crane-hire services vary from place to place, so just in case the crane is normally only used for building or industrial work, find out in advance whether they or you will supply the slings and spreaders; they can normally be borrowed or hired from a boatyard.

As I mentioned, the operator will almost certainly know how to do his job, and will probably not appreciate being treated as though he doesn't, so a fairly diplomatic approach will be necessary. All the same, it is your boat, and you are paying for a service.

When the boat is lifted from the trailer the boat is bound to swing one way or the other—unless the operator is so good that he has managed to position his jib exactly above the central point of the boat, which is well-nigh impossible. In some instances there may be enough all-round clearance for this not to matter, but usually it is best to steady the boat by previously tying a rope at the bow and stern and having a person on the ground at either end to hold on. This way a vicious swing can easily be stopped. The only problem is that your naked hull will generally have nothing on the deck to which a rope can be fastened, and this is another reason to make sure that the boat arrives before the crane, and that you are on hand with your steps to climb up and fasten a couple of galvanized eye bolts, if there is nothing more convenient to which your rope can be tied.

This mostly applies to GRP hulls, because steel hulls will usually have some cleats or Samson-posts already welded in place, and ferro hulls will have pre-cast holes through which a rope can be run. Unless there is a force nine blowing, the strain should be minimal.

When drilling the holes for the eye bolts, try and place them where they will either eventually be covered, or where you will need a hole anyway. It will only take a few minutes with a brace and a sharp half-inch bit.

Eye bolts are better at this stage because they are cheap, only need one hole, and you won't need to bother too much about positioning. The cleats you will eventually fit will need more careful planning for position, and will have to be fitted properly, so they are best left until you reach that stage.

Without giving you time to grow more than a few grey hairs a crane driver, maybe with some assistance from you placing the slings and spreaders, will smartly pluck your dream ship off the lorry and lower it gently onto the cradle or bilge-keels, and all the panic will be over.

While he has your boat suspended in mid-air, ask the driver the weight of the hull as it stands—if his crane is the normal type with a weight gauge on it. It will be interesting to compare this with its weight when it is finally craned into the water to see how much you have added. There is also another reason, which I will go into shortly.

For now, however, as soon as you are satisfied the boat is sitting comfortably, and unlikely to fall over, your next priority should be to take your helper(s) into the nearest hostelry for a drink, which you will need much more than they do. When the tension has drained away and you are able to think coherently again, you will be better able to remember all the things you have to do before you are finished for the day, like erecting a shelter, or tying a tarpaulin over the cockpit to stop it filling up with rain-water. Very soon you will have to start glassing in bulkheads, for which dryness is of paramount importance.

3 · The work begins

Working with GRP

A great deal of fitting out any type of hull is similar in many ways, whatever the material, the major difference being the method of attaching bulkheads etc., to the shell.

A lot of the following pages will therefore apply to all types, even though they are directed at GRP. Variations for steel and ferro-cement will be dealt with in a later chapter.

Whatever you buy will reflect, to some extent, the amount you pay for it. GRP hulls are no exception, and because of this, the less you pay for it probably means the more you will have to do to it.

Due to the increasing trend towards home completion, many hulls are now being built specifically for this market, giving the builder as little to do as possible. Most of the hull stiffness, for example, will already have been bonded in, leaving only the addition of bulkheads, structurally speaking, to be added.

In fact, depending on your time and money situation, as I mentioned earlier, you have the choice of starting fairly near the beginning, or well towards the end. For the purpose of this book I will assume that you are starting from the beginning, i.e. a basic hull, without superstructure or any form of stiffening, ballast etc.

At this point it might be worth repeating that once at sea, if that is where you aim to end up, the stresses your hull will be subjected to will, at times, be quite severe. This being so, the job has to be done right if it is not to fall apart just when you need it most. The sea is a potentially dangerous environment and is unsympathetic to faulty workmanship. This should be borne in mind by those who feel inclined to start off with a basic hull merely because it is the cheapest available.

With your hull the manufacturer will normally provide drawings showing the location of stringers, bulkheads etc., and these should be

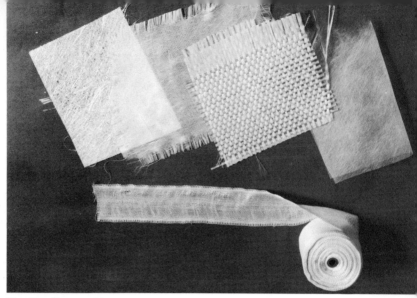

10: Glassfibre materials

followed carefully, because the designer knows best where the strength needs adding. Should you wish to alter the interior layout significantly, consult the designer first. The re-positioning of a bulkhead might be quite feasible, but on the other hand, it could remove strength from where it is vital.

The first time I clambered into the hull of my initial attempt at fitting out a boat, I was struck by the enormity of the task so casually taken on. My first reaction was one of near panic—where on earth should I start? It looked so incredibly empty and totally divorced from the two-dimensional drawings with which I had become so familiar. I might add that this sensation returned when I entered my second hull for the first time, so fight down the feeling of alarm, things will be better soon.

Right, your hull has been delivered, levelled off on a nice, solid bed (*see* Fig. 8), and is sitting firmly in the building cradle. A shelter is keeping the elements at bay and access steps or stairs are in position. In other words, you are ready to begin.

Your first, and many subsequent tasks will involve the use of GRP for bonding in stringers, bulkheads, shelves etc., so it will be necessary to have a knowledge of the materials and how to use them.

Nearly everyone who writes about the use of GRP seems to use different techniques, tools and materials, which can be a bit baffling to the beginner. The reason for this is the large range of materials available, many of which do the same job; this also applies to tools, and builders always evolve their own techniques with the use of both.

A glance at a supplier's list will show nine or ten different types of glass matt or tape. It will also show that price is largely dependent on quantity. Apart from one or two specialized jobs we will come to later,

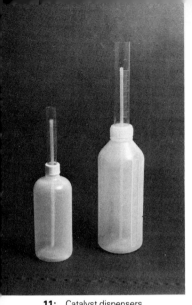

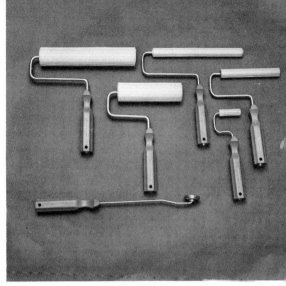

11: Catalyst dispensers   **12:** Various GRP laminating rollers

1½-oz CSM (chopped strand matt) can be used throughout your building project. It is sold either by length or weight, and the manufacturer of your hull can give you some idea of how much to buy, so you may be able to take advantage of a quantity discount.

Clear, pre-accelerated polyester resin will do 99% if not all the job, so the same applies.

It is possible to make a saving by buying resin and accelerator separately, but unless you are familiar with the products or chemically knowledgeable this is not to be recommended. The reason for this is that catalyst and accelerator will ignite or explode if brought into direct contact, whereas pre-accelerated resin and catalyst can be mixed quite safely. The small saving isn't worth the possible consequences unless you have the know-how.

Catalyst is sold as liquid or paste; this is another matter of personal preference. I prefer it in liquid form because a dispenser may then be used to ensure accurate quantities.

Bonding paste for gluing stringers etc. to the shell, preparatory to glassing them in, may be made up by adding an industrial talc to resin (pre-accelerated) and then adding catalyst when you come to use it, or it can be purchased ready-mixed.

Fillers can also be made up this way, or bought as proprietary brands such as Isopon, Tetrosil, or Cataloy.

Some builders thin down resin with a ten to twelve per cent addition of styrene for priming areas of foam, ply etc. to be bonded to GRP, others just use a straight resin catalyst mix.

Acetone will be needed for pre-cleaning areas to be bonded, and for cleaning tools after use.

Tools for working with GRP are fortunately quite cheap and basic.

Apart from soft rollers and brushes, in fact, only two other actual tools are necessary; a choice of two types of roller for compacting the lamination and squeezing out trapped air bubbles, and either a trimming knife or wallpaper type scissors for cutting the CSM to the desired size.

A lot of people advocate the use of lambswool rollers for both 'wetting out' and rolling the sections into position. Others, including myself, prefer to use a brush for this part of the operation. My own reason for this preference is that I find rollers tend to become too saturated with resin and use too much acetone when being cleaned out.

I hasten to add that this is a purely personal opinion, probably brought about by the fact that I started off using brushes, which is most likely why I find them handier.

The tool I use most during a 'glassing' session is the type of metal roller which is like a gear wheel in section, often known as a paddle roller. These come in various sizes, but for the sort of smallish areas you will be working on, a paddle about three inches in length and one inch in diameter is a good general size. Another popular type of roller is based on a row of washers spaced alternately by smaller washers. Both types can be dismantled for cleaning, a useful asset as any amount of sloshing around in the acetone never quite seems to remove every trace of resin, and this results in the roller seizing up every now and then.

If the roller is all metal, it is possible to get rid of the accumulated resin by burning it away with a blowlamp, but some have nylon spacers, so stripping down is the only way. If you use the blowlamp method, keep the wind behind you or use a mask to avoid breathing the highly toxic fumes, and make sure that you do it where any pieces of burning resin that fall off do so harmlessly.

To complete the necessary gear you will need various pots for mixing resin and for an acetone bath for brush and roller cleaning, and finally, a 'wetting out' board.

The type of pot I have found most useful is the half-gallon polythene container that white spirit is sold in, with the top cut off (a trimming knife will do this very easily). The result is a translucent, flexible pot which can be marked to ensure the correct quantity of resin is used each time, and flexed to break out any old resin which has hardened inside. It is useful to have two of these on the go, because it is much easier to remove resin after it has cured and you may not want to wait that long.

The same type of pot can be used for acetone, and again it is useful to have two. For this use I prefer to cut out only the front section (*see* photo 12a) because this leaves you with a handle for portability. A piece of chicken wire pushed in to one pot, bent down at the edges to keep it about an inch off the bottom, will keep brushes and rollers immersed, but clear of the congealing resin which will collect underneath. A measure of acetone in the other pot can be used for the initial sloshing around the cleaning so the implements can be fairly free from resin when left to soak in the other.

An acetone will eventually evaporate, tools for long-term storage should be thoroughly cleaned in it, washed out in hot water and detergent, rinsed in clear water, and then left to dry. Resin is amazingly tenuous, and once mixed with catalyst, it will cure enough to clog up a roller or ruin a brush if just left in the bottom of an acetone pot unsuspended by mesh, or in water, so a proper cleaning system is essential if brushes and rollers are not constantly to be renewed.

Acetone (or nail-varnish remover) will destroy GRP if left in contact for long enough. Small splashes will usually evaporate before any harm is done, but major spillage could result in considerable damage, so if you leave open pots of acetone in the boat take great care to put them where they cannot be accidentally knocked over and left unnoticed. If you do spill any, mop it up thoroughly. If possible, do the cleaning off the boat and leave the open pots in a protected position underneath it on the ground out of harm's way and out of the reach of young children etc.

A sheet of formica about three feet by one foot will make a good 'wetting out' board. As with the polythene pot, this may be flexed to break away hardened resin and therefore present a clean working surface again. Although not so flexible, a piece of GRP from the boat (such as a window cut-out) is quite suitable as long as the gelcoat remains unscratched, so take care when scraping clean. The more scored the surface becomes the better resin will stick to it. As it will

12a: Plastic container for brushes, before and after cutting with a trimming knife

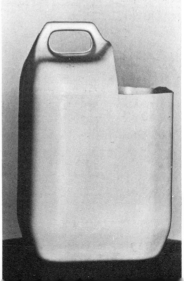

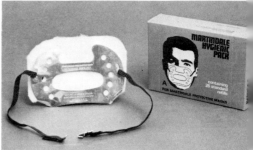

13: Respirator   **14:** Face mask

eventually become too lumpy to use, save all your large cut-outs for future wetting out boards.

Always wear expendable clothes when glassing. It may be possible to do the job without getting covered in the stuff, but I have never yet managed to find anyone who has done so. After a few sessions it is quite normal for trousers to be leant against a wall rather than folded over a chair. Not everyone finds them comfortable to wear like this, so eventually replacement is inevitable.

Being such a good material for boats, i.e. waterproof, unaffected by changes in temperature etc., also makes cured resin impossible to wash off clothes.

Before starting the job, there are a few safety aspects to bear in mind when working with GRP and associated chemicals.

The fumes given off by curing resin are toxic. They seem to affect some more than others, but however well you feel able to cope, avoid

15: Modern GRP factory and equipment in use

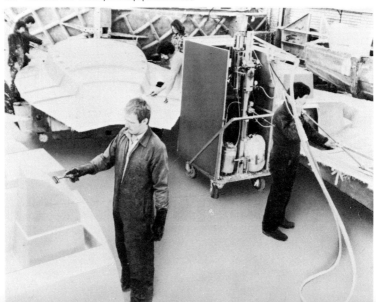

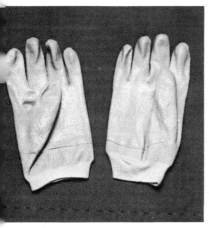

17: Protective plastic gloves

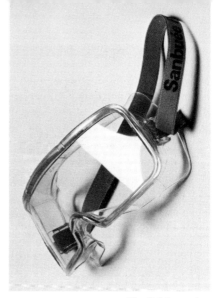

16: Safety goggles

working for too long in an unventilated situation. Apart from nausea and a state akin to drunkenness, should you stay with it too long, it is also possible to achieve a condition very similar to the 'bends' or nitrogen narcosis experienced by deep sea divers who ascend too quickly. The resulting cramps can be very painful and take some hours to recede.

To avoid this, always ensure the best possible air circulation, and where this is still inadequate come up for fresh air regularly.

Manufacturers have extractor and fresh air pumping facilities which obviate the fume problem, but these are a bit elaborate for the average amateur. Nevertheless, if you are one of the unfortunate ones who is affected quite badly, even by short spells in the fumes, a portable compressor and a length of pipe leading into the boat can do a lot to alleviate the problem.

Protection to the skin and especially the eyes is very important and frequently ignored, sometimes with tragic results. Should you get splashed in the eyes by resin, or even worse, catalyst, rinse immediately with copious amounts of water and then seek medical attention for proper cleansing. Failure to do this can result in permanent damage. It is not that difficult to get an eyeful, especially when glassing above your head, so use goggles where necessary. The drips that eventually render them opaque will be proof of what might have gone in your eyes.

Heavy duty rubber gloves will protect the hands completely, but a surprising amount of people refuse to wear them because they make the hands feel clumsy and they can be uncomfortable in hot weather when you sweat inside them. Whilst I agree with both these points of view, my advice is perseverance. The feeling of clumsiness will soon go to a certain extent, and in any case, although glassing needs care it is not a precision operation that demands fingertip sensitivity.

Dusting the inside of the gloves with talc will help the sweating, and any further discomfort felt pales beside the excruciating pain of filing a build-up of hardened resin from the fingernails and going down too far.

If you do get resin all over your hands it is best to clean it off, before it has cured, with a proprietary brand of resin removing cream rather than acetone, as the latter also removes essential oils from your skin which often results in dermatitis.

Should you really find gloves impossible, a generous application of barrier cream and a dusting of talc will help to some extent. Cover any cuts with waterproof plaster first, if catalyst gets into an open wound the pain can bring tears to the eyes of the bravest amongst us.

Finally, when you mix up a quantity of pre-accelerated resin and catalyst, a chemical reaction will begin to warm the mixture up. Spread out in the normal way; this results in a cure over a period of twenty minutes or so, depending on the temperature and the amount of catalyst added. If left in too great a quantity, however, the heat build-up escalates until it may eventually ignite. For this reason, avoid mixing more than you can use, and if for any reason you mix up a batch and then get called away for an urgent phone call or whatever, remember to take the pot off the boat with you, and pour it out where it will do no harm. Wasteful maybe, but better than a bonfire on board in your absence.

All this probably makes the fitting out of a GRP hull sound too dangerous to contemplate, which is, of course, nonsense. A lot of people have been doing it for many years without coming to any harm at all. It pays to be aware of hazards to avoid them.

A roll of twenty-five yards or more of CSM is quite heavy to handle, and as it will be weeks or months before you finish it, it is bound to get damaged or at least dirty if just left lying around. In a small hull it can also get in the way. For these reasons it pays to make a suitable dispenser (*see* Fig. 1) from which it may be hung and used conveniently. A broomstick and a few scraps of timber with suffice.

As a couple of final hints before you actually start, try and persuade a mate to do the 'wetting out' (process to be described in a minute). With one person doing the mixing and wetting out, and the other doing the laying up, the job can be done at least twice as quickly as doing it all alone, and it means you will be clear of the fumes sooner. Also, use a few pieces of boarding to make one or two level surfaces to sit on, do the mixing on etc. Unless you are building a flat-bottomed craft, gravity will be your constant enemy at this stage, and much of your energy will be taken up trying to defy it. On some deep keel hulls

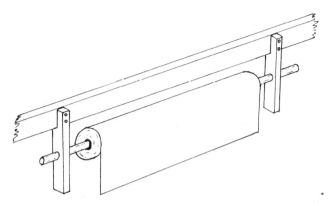

Fig. 1: CSM Dispenser, made from 2″ × 1″ deal fastened to any suitable beam or stiffener, using a broomstick as a roller

the tendency to keep sliding downwards can be really exasperating when you need your hands free to work with.

The preparation for doing a glassing job is much the same as any other work where adhesives are used. All surfaces have to be clean and dry, and free from dust and grease. They also need to be well keyed (roughened up). In this way a good mechanical bond can be achieved.

Because of the limited 'pot life' of resin once the catalyst has been added, a certain amount of planning is necessary to avoid wastage. If there are two of you for example, make sure the mixer doesn't overtake the 'layer upper'. Although it is desirable to do the job as quickly as possible, it must be done thoroughly, so if the two of you are out of sight of each other, which often happens when the 'layer upper' is working under the cockpit or in some other inaccessible place, be sure to keep your mate informed of progress so that the wetted out strips of CSM are handed to you at a manageable rate.

Another point to bear in mind is that the strips of wetted out CSM will drip resin while they are being passed to the working area, so if this might spoil a surface which will eventually be visible, make sure to protect it.

The act of roughing up the surfaces to provide a key is bound to create dust, especially if done with a coarse grit sanding disc on a drill or angle grinder, and this must be removed before you start. If you have power, a cylinder type vacuum cleaner is useful for this job.

Before going into details, a suitable order of working is as follows:

1 Key the surfaces to be glassed.
2 Remove dust.
3 Cut strips of CSM, enough for immediate needs.
4 Wipe GRP surfaces to be glassed with acetone.

5 Mix required quantity of resin and catalyst.
6 Paint area to be glassed with resin.
7 Wet out CSM strips (one at a time).
8 Position CSM strip and roll out trapped air.
9 Repeat 7 and 8, overlapping each strip by two or three inches.

The above list is not meant to describe any specific glassing job. These will be covered shortly. Obviously you may want to modify the order to suit certain jobs, but a system is important.

Taking the list step by step; in providing a key on GRP, the idea is to expose at least some strands of glass under the surface coat of resin. If you use a power tool, be sure to wear goggles and a dust mask. Should you find a power supply is impossible at this stage, the job can be done by muscle power using a coarse production paper followed by scoring lines in all directions with a sharp point. Resin will blunt most things very quickly, so a ceramic tile scorer with a tungsten tip is useful here.

Areas of wood to be glassed should be made as rough as possible, and in addition to scratching, lots of holes an eighth to a quarter of an inch deep will help adhesion. These can be made with a hammer and a three- or four-inch nail, or an electric drill with an eighth- or three-sixteenth bit. In the case of bulkheads a neat job can be achieved with the help of a router. The edge to be glassed is routered down to the intended thickness of the CSM strips, and about three inches inwards (*see* Fig. 2). This is not essential, but makes future trimming a bit easier.

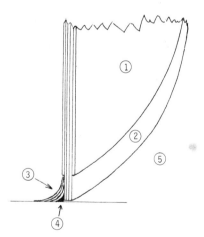

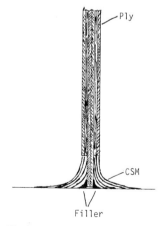

Fig. 2: 1. Bulkhead 2. Routered edge 3. Layers of CSM 4. Filler 5. Hull

Fig. 3

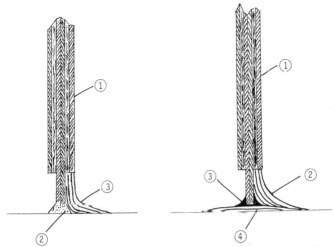

Fig. 3a: 1. Ply bulkhead   2. Foam
strip   3. CSM

Fig. 3b: 1. Ply bulkhead   2. CSM
3. Filler   4. CSM

When cutting the CSM strips, a little care can make the end result look a lot better. Keep the edges as straight as possible; this may obviate trimming before a complete cure is effected. The latter can need to be done at an inconvenient time (and it won't wait, because it must be done while the CSM is still 'green' i.e. not fully hardened), and clumsy trimming can result in lifting the CSM from the wood and thus spoiling adhesion.

Don't cut the strips too long, or they become difficult to handle when wetted out, especially when working upwards on the underneath of decks or coachroofs etc.

Sometimes the strips need to be of varying widths so that each successive layer overlaps the previous one by an inch or so to spread the load and provide a taper (*see* Fig. 3). In this event keep each pile of strips separate, and let your partner, should you have one, know which you want next. Don't let the dry strips come into contact with mixed resin, or this will harden and they will be useless.

Wiping the surface with acetone will remove all traces of wax and grease, and 'liven up' the GRP for a better bond.

The mixture of resin and catalyst depends on the temperature in which you are working. On a hot summer's day a one per cent addition of catalyst will give a 'pot life' of around twenty minutes before beginning to 'gel', at which time it should be considered expendable. In cooler conditions up to four per cent will be necessary to achieve the same result. More than four per cent and the mixture will become too hot and tend to be brittle when cured, also it will give you very little time in which to work. Too little catalyst will result in the mixture never curing properly. When this happens the surface will remain tacky to the touch, and will need painting over with a 'hot' mix (around four per cent) to cure it.

Although not critical, it will be seen that mixing needs a certain amount of care, and if conditions are too cold i.e. under 60 degrees Fahrenheit (about 16 centigrade) some form of artificial heat will become necessary.

To help measure out quantities, between 5 and 10 ccs of catalyst should be added to each pound of pre-accelerated resin (an average teaspoon holds around 5 ccs). It will be best to weigh out the first batch on the kitchen scales (suitably protected from resin drips) and mark the mixing pots accordingly.

Make sure to stir the catalyst in well, after which the mixture can be used for priming the area to be glassed immediately prior to wetting out the CSM.

The strands of glass in CSM are held together by a mild bonding agent and it takes the resin a minute or so to dissolve this and make the CSM become supple and workable, so don't worry if the strip feels a little stiff to begin with.

Slosh some resin on to the wetting-out board with a brush, lay the strip on the resin and paint on more resin working it in to the CSM but avoiding tearing it apart. When the first side is wet, turn it over and repeat the process. It doesn't need to be really saturated, just impregnated.

The act of turning it over, and lifting it off the wetting-out board can be a bit tricky at first, as part of the strip may tend to stick to the board. This is usually solved by laying it down again and lifting it from the opposite end. It depends which way the 'weave' in the CSM goes.

The wetted-out strip is then handed to the 'layer upper' if there is one, who will position it and roll it into place, eliminating all the trapped air-pockets at the same time. Although some people favour stippling the strip into position with a brush, the crackle of bursting air bubbles heard when you follow up immediately with a roller is proof enough that a brush is not good enough on its own.

Ballast

Before anything is built into the hull, while it is completely open and accessible, is the best time to add the necessary ballast.

In a general book such as this, it is impossible to describe the ballasting of every type of boat, or the best material to use. This information, however, may be of vital importance for your boat, and so if not already supplied with the shell and plans, contact the manufacturer for details.

In the majority of GRP sailing boats, the ballast is 'encapsulated', that is, it is added to the inside of the hollow keel moulding and then sealed in place.

Some motor boats, of whatever material, need a limited amount of internal ballast, and the easiest answer may simply be the addition of concrete, which is often added to a pre-applied layer of pitch, to seal the steel, wood etc. underneath. Alternatively, loose iron pigs may be wedged into the designed space.

In GRP monohull sailing boats, where a lot of weight needs to be put low down, more precision is usually necessary. It is important that all the specified weight fits into the keel moulding, or the balance and centre of gravity of the boat may be adversely affected, and the addition of more ballast in the bilge area may prohibit the use of under floor tanks etc.

In most cases the manufacturer, or at least the designer, will be able to tell you exactly how much ballast to add. Allowance for later additions of weight such as fuel and water will almost certainly have been accounted for.

Concrete is nothing like as heavy as solid cast-iron or lead, and iron pigs or scrap will usually be unsuitable as the space between them will detract from the overall weight.

To combat this, it is essential to use small particles that will pack down effectively.

Lead is the obvious answer, being very dense and non-corrosive, but this is usually ruled out by the price.

Washer pressings, the small steel discs removed from the centre of washers, are often suitable, but as they are liable to rust, care should be taken to put them in dry, and do a good sealing job.

The amount of ballast you add should be carefully weighed out, a process which has meant the premature demise of more than one set of bathroom scales, and a note kept as you go along. Mixing each bucketful with resin knits it all nicely together, but beware adding too much at once in case the mixture gets too hot. For safety's sake, add it in thin layers, using a weak resin/catalyst mix, and let each layer 'go off' before adding the next. Between 4″ and 6″ at a time is usually all right, depending on the outside temperature.

The large GRP suppliers will advise you on this subject, and as progress in development of plastics is going ahead all the time, it is sound policy to write for the latest information. There are casting resins available which can be more suitable for this particular job. Firms such as Martins Plastics and Strand Glassfibre, whose addresses appear in the Appendix at the back of the book, produce leaflets detailing all aspects of GRP and its various uses.

Another firm, Barton Abrasives, supplies all the necessary ingredients in their product 'Ballast-Pak'. This is specifically aimed at the

DIY market for ballasting internal keels, and is approved by Lloyds. This is a complete system, which has the added convenience of obtaining all the necessary materials from one place.

The aft end of the keel will be the usual place for the pumping well. Normally the lowest part of the boat, this is where any accumulated bilge-water will drain back to. Bearing this in mind, and the desirability to clear all the bilge-water without leaving puddles, the final layer should be nice and smooth. It is a good idea to mould in a small well for a submersible pump to sit in at this point and thereby create a definite collection point.

Bonding hull to deck and superstructure

My own preference is for this job to be done by the manufacturer, because this will ensure that the boat is fairly strong and better able to stand up to transport and craning. In addition, a large deck and superstructure unit in GRP is very heavy, and will often have to be raised so that a bedding layer can be applied to the joint.

With some shells, the latter is already done, and the two units are bolted together, merely leaving you with the job of internal bonding.

Make sure you know what you will be faced with if you intend doing it all yourself, and don't be afraid to ask the correct procedure from the manufacturer.

Where internal bonding is necessary, the process is as already described. In places, especially where a cockpit unit is fitted, the joints will be quite inaccessible, and considerable contortions will be needed to reach them all, nevertheless, they must be reached as they are all of immense importance. Also, at least half of the CSM you are laying up will be upside down, so you have gravity to contend with as well. Two or three layers of 1½-oz CSM, spread for five or six inches either side of the join will probably be needed, but make sure to check on the recommendations for your particular boat. CSM cannot follow sharp corners, or be pushed into narrow recesses, so if the toe-rail moulding, for instance, produces these shapes, they will have to be filled and radiused before you start. Large recesses which would use expensive quantities of filler can be filled with polyurethane foam strips first.

Hull stiffeners

Some hulls need stiffeners to provide longitudinal support, especially around the turn of the bilge where there may be large flattish areas, vulnerable to flexing.

If they are recommended for your hull, you can make a considerable saving by bonding them in yourself, and they should be installed before the bulkheads.

Sometimes called stringers, they are most suitably made from strips of polyurethane foam, as these can be purchased ready-shaped in pre-cut lengths.

Positions, which should be indicated on the drawings or found out, should be marked on the inside of the hull, the lengths of foam stuck into place using the proprietary adhesive supplied by a GRP firm, or resin stiffened to a paste with industrial talc (from the same source) and then catalyst added as the paste is needed. Once stuck, any gaps and discrepancies can be filled with the same paste, and smoothed over. Now paint the foam and the area to be bonded with a normal resin mix with ten per cent styrene (again from the same source) which will put a good bonding surface on the foam, allow to dry, then glass in as already described.

Extra strength can be gained by sandwiching a layer of woven rovings, or woven tape in-between two layers of CSM.

18: Polyurethane foam stringers being glassed into the hull

If foam strips are unavailable, the same effect can be created by using cardboard tubing or even rolled up newspaper held by tape. It is the GRP that provides the strength.

Care should be taken to angle the top edges so as not to create water traps, or to provide a channel where water might collect up against a bulkhead when fitted.

Bulkheads

Bulkheads are walls in the house sense, which create divisions or compartments. The first major job, after the ballast, and stiffeners if necessary, will be the main bulkheads. The position of these will be marked on the drawing, and in a typical boat they will often divide the forward berth compartment from the saloon area, sometimes with a

19:   A bulkhead bonded into the hull

20: A bulkhead being laminated into the hull directly onto glassed-in foam frames and stringers. Note the use of masking tape to protect woodwork that will show later

head and shower in-between, and then the saloon from the cockpit. Smaller boats, where the saloon and forward cabin is one and the same, will often need only two, or perhaps even one main bulkhead.

In the next chapter is a description of fitting bulkheads to a hull only, and although basically the same operation, it is much easier without a 'roof' on, where a large area of heavy ply may be lowered into position and hung vertically for attaching to the skin. Where the deck and superstructure is already in place, the width of ply you can fit in one piece will depend on the size of the access into the shell, and where there is a GRP cockpit moulding, this can be quite restricted. This is not so much a disadvantage structurally, because except in the case of very small boats, ply sheets aren't wide enough to form a full-width bulkhead anyway, so sections usually need joining, and the joins can normally be positioned to form doorways etc. The disadvantage is felt more when struggling inside with the section and trying to hold it in place for fastening whilst defying gravity and the curvature of the hull at the same time.

Forgetting these traumas for the moment, let us first consider the two methods of attachment: (a) where stiffeners are already bonded in, and (b) where the bulkhead is fastened direct to the skin.

For both methods, bulkhead sections will have to be measured and cut (*see* Fig. 4), and marks will have to be made on the hull to determine the exact position (Figs. 5 & 6). More on this later.

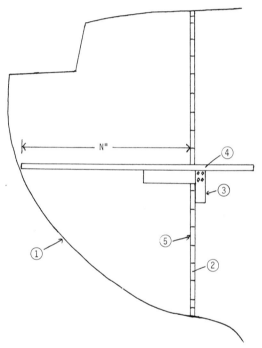

Fig. 4:   1. Hull   2. Batten, marked in 3″ or 6″ sections as appropriate with curvature
3. Square   4. Batten   5. Extent of bulkhead

Although a bulkhead may be made from ¾″ ply, the edge must be considered sharp where it makes contact with the hull. Because of this, precautions have to be taken to ensure that stress, or shrinkage of GRP in the bonding process doesn't raise high spots which would not only be a potential weakness, but would also be unsightly when viewed from outside.

(a) Where stiffeners are in place, they will do the job of spreading the load a bulkhead may impart over a wide area of the hull. There is

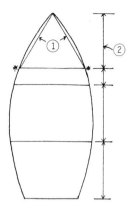

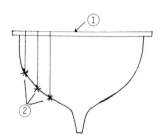

Fig. 5: Marking bulkhead positions
1. Equidistant lengths from centre of
bow to mark gunwales
2. Dimensions as in plan

Fig. 6: Marking bulkhead positions
1. Beam laid on gunwale marks   2.
Marks determined by plumb-line

therefore no need to cut the bulkhead around them, but merely to rest it against them (*see* Fig. 7), fill the resultant gaps with foam strips, and bond the bulkhead to the hull using progressively wider strips of CSM to achieve a neat taper (*see* Fig. 3a).

(b) Without stiffeners the load may be spread in three ways, depending on the thickness of the hull. Where this is very robust, i.e. ½″ or more, either method (i) or (ii) will be sufficient.

(i) Cut the ply roughly to shape; accuracy against the hull is not critical, so gaps up to about ½″ are all right.

Using a quarter-inch ply offcut, a few inches long and with a 1½″ radius at one end, squeeze filler down the bonding edge, pressing it into any gaps, and ending up with a nice, smooth radius on both sides

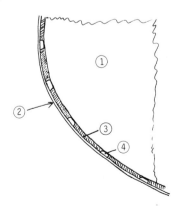

Fig. 7:   1. Bulkhead   2. Hull   3. Foam strips   4. Stiffeners

of the bulkhead (*see* Fig. 3). As soon as the filler has cured (ten minutes or so in around 60 degrees Fahrenheit), the whole lot can be bounded to the hull, using increasing widths of CSM as before, and spreading out up to six inches either side of the bulkhead to spread the load well.

(ii) The same basic process, but with the bulkhead cut an inch undersize, and a foam strip used as a cushion (*see* Fig. 3a).

(iii) The same process as (i), but where the hull is on the thin side, it is advisable to thicken it up a few inches either side of where the bulkhead will go by glassing in a couple of layers of CSM (*see* Fig. 3b).

Positioning a bulkhead for bonding

The inside of a shell, especially a curvaceous one, is a bewildering place to begin determining straight lines, so it is necessary to start from basics.

Provided the hull is level athwart and the water-line is horizontal (method as in Fig. 8), as should have been done by now, then a plumb-line suspended from the deckhead will be vertical when the boat is afloat, so any bulkhead fastened around plumbed marks will be absolutely upright after launching with the boat properly trimmed.

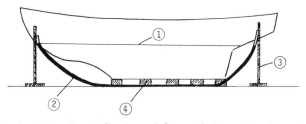

Fig. 8: 1. Water-line   2. Clear hose   3. Supports for hose   4. Level supports

The bulkhead also has to be at right angles to the fore and aft centreline, and this can be done by measurement from the centre of the stem as high up as possible (*see* Fig. 5).

The drawing should show the straight line measurement from the stem to the first bulkhead, and after that the distance between each bulkhead to follow. Brace a straight piece of 2″ × 1″ across the shell, hard up under the decks, so that the forward edge corresponds to the measurement on the drawing when each end is equidistant from the stem.

The forward edge of the batten will now represent the centreline of the bulkhead when viewed from above, and it is now only necessary to make a series of marks on the hull to correspond with this line, and this can be done with a plumb-line.

Unless you have very long arms, a mate is very useful at this point either to hold the plumb-line or make the marks. The idea is to hold the line on the deckhead so that it just kisses the forward edge of the batten, and make a mark top and bottom. A repetition of this process all the way across the boat at regular intervals will ensure that the bulkhead, or each section of it, goes in square.

Once you have made the marks, it is of great importance that the bulkhead follows them when attached. I know this sounds like stating the obvious, but it is not always that simple to wedge it firmly in position for bonding, and keep it in that position once you have started work on it. It is on the cards that callers may arrive just as you have carefully propped it in place, cause the boat to shake as they clamber up the ladder, and make it especially difficult for you to be polite. Apart from anything else, the bottom edge of a collapsing bulkhead always seems to catch you on the shins.

There are numerous ways of alleviating this problem, depending on the shape of the hull. In fairly flat hulls it will be a lot easier to wedge top and bottom (making sure you are not forcing a bend into the ply). In deep 'V' configurations or deep-keel sailing boats there is usually nothing to stop a section obeying the call of gravity. A batten such as the one you used for 'plumbing' will help, if it is secure, as the ply may be held to it with a G-cramp. A good method is to bond temporarily small right-angle brackets around the marks in three or four places (³⁄₈″ away from the marks a ¾″ bulkhead etc.), bend the upright part vertical if necessary, and screw the bulkhead in place until the initial bonding has been done. This method is useful when you want to hold the bulkhead clear of the hull to insert filler or foam.

Once one section is bonded, subsequent sections or bulkheads will always be easier to prop up by using battens, G-cramps and pins etc., also, their positioning may be measured from the first one.

Cutting and preparing the ply

The easiest method is to wedge a floor to ceiling batten, plumbed vertical, down what will be the edge of the bulkhead section (if you are using standard size sheets, this will often be four feet in from the side).

Mark this batten every three inches, and using a set square and straight-edge, measure from each mark to the hull (*see* Fig. 4), noting each measurement in pencil against the relevant mark on the batten. With the batten laid close to the edge of the ply for reference, the measurements can be transferred by exactly the same method (square and straight-edge), the resulting marks joined together and then cut out with a jigsaw, after double checking!

As described in the next section, it is not a bad idea to start with a hardboard template. This only needs to be the size of the largest section to be made, and can then be cut down for each smaller one in turn.

Before preparing the bonding equipment, the bulkhead should be 'offered up' to check for a fit, and the edge to be bonded should be well scored and given lots of hammered or drilled indentations up to about three inches inwards where the CSM is to adhere.

If you have a router, this three inches can be chewed out down to a depth of an eighth of an inch or so each side. This provides a good bonding surface and saves the CSM from forming a step on the ply (*see* Fig. 2).

Where the bulkhead crosses the lowest point of the keel, make limber holes for water drainage (described later in chapter 4, Fig. 15).

Finally, the foam used for bedding a bulkhead or forming a stiffener must be polyurethane, polystyrene will just dissolve when brought into contact with polyester resin.

Deviations from the drawing

Minor alterations in bulkhead positions are often feasible, to make a compartment larger or smaller as you desire, but *not* where mast support is involved. Where you wish to make substantial changes, consult the designer or manufacturer.

4 · Design and carpentry

Fitting bulkheads, decks and coachroofs

Carpentry used in boat building can be quite complex, or it can be kept relatively simple. If you have a good knowledge of the subject, access to machinery and plenty of time, then you will probably manage this side of your task without my help.

On the other hand, if you lack the know-how, but your interest in joinery and cabinet work outweighs your hurry to begin sailing, and you intend to dovetail all the drawers etc., a more advanced book than this will be needed. One that specializes in the subject.

For this book I intend to deal with basic methods of adequate strength. I might add that this is in no way to decry refinements, which can be very satisfying both visually and therapeutically as well as very strong, but they do take time and/or expensive equipment.

Simple joints bonded with modern adhesives provide great strength, need not look unsightly and in many cases will be hidden by panelling or facing of some kind when the job is finished.

For those ambitious souls who are starting from the basic hull only, to set out by constructing a ply dinghy will definitely pay dividends. The plans you buy will explain diagrammatically all the joints and building methods and by the time you have finished you will have a fair idea of how to build a deck and coachroof. The methods are essentially the same, maybe varying in scantlings (size and thickness of materials).

The first consideration is the design. If this is bad, there is little chance of the finished product looking otherwise. A look around the yards and moorings will show you workboat conversions or hull completions of many varying standards. Some are well up to professional standard, where the superstructure forms a sleek and aesthetic extension of the hull, and others would be more suitable as garden sheds.

To be fair, a good proportion of the latter are on static houseboats or inland cruisers, but not all, and in any case a design in keeping with the hull is often just as easy to build, and must at least help the resale value even on a houseboat.

For offshore use, of course, the strength factor can be vital to the safety of the crew, making a sound design of utmost importance. Panoramic windows in large, flat areas of ply can be nice from the inside, providing light and spacious accommodation, but such surfaces are prone to sudden and dramatic removal under the force of breaking waves. High sides also promote windage problems causing leeway when sailing, and make confined mooring manoeuvres hazardous to say the least.

With very few exceptions stock production boats look right. This isn't always noticeable because it is usually only bad designs that shout at you and offend the eye. The good ones should look suitable for their purpose whether that is fishing or offshore racing.

The reason for the good looks of most production boats is that they have been designed by skilled naval architects who are well aware of the strength needed for a given usage and able to combine this with handsome lines.

To produce your own superstructure design it is usually best to start with sketches. Take two or three sheets of paper and draw the side view of the hull on each, using a simple scale such as one inch, or perhaps half an inch to the foot. Now draw in two or three alternative cabin tops, lightly, so they can be rubbed out or modified. It will soon be apparent that some look better than others.

For the reasons already stated it is best to stick to standard shapes, sizes, heights etc. Boring though it may seem, radical departures in shape are usually unsuitable.

Starting from a bare hull does give you some scope for alteration—a centre cockpit instead of an aft cockpit, for example, or a longer coachroof to give more internal space. For fishing, it may be desirable to sacrifice accommodation for a large, open cockpit.

Probably the biggest design problem on small craft under, say, eight metres, is to obtain satisfactory standing headroom below decks. This applies especially to small sailing craft where cabin sides must be kept low for seaworthiness and stability.

In the smaller boats it is sometimes just not possible, and it is best to make sure that at least good sitting headroom is available.

On many catamarans, where the saloon area is generally situated on the bridge deck, standing room is only feasible in the hulls. This is not such a disadvantage as it may seem; saloons are for sitting in. The important areas for full height are the companion-ways, or 'walk throughs' from one part of the accommodation to another, the galley, where a stooping cook is likely to be an unwilling cook (or even a maimed cook in a seaway!) and if possible, the head (toilet compartment).

On very small boats the galley and head are often matters for ingenuity; for example, they can be situated directly below sliding or lifting hatches, or skylights, to gain those few vital inches that may make all the difference between comfort and abject misery.

So it will be seen that headroom, whilst a desirable commodity, should not be attained by just building upwards regardless.

Deck area is another factor directly affecting the accommodation. Wide side decks are obviously preferable for working on, but may seriously interfere with even sitting headroom below, so normally a compromise is necessary. Some designs have flush decks to alleviate this problem. This is where there are no side decks, the main deck running from gunwale to gunwale. Where the hull is not designed for this, however, the hull sides will have to be extended upwards for a foot or so from the forward end of the cockpit to the bow.

I have known this to be done satisfactorily in GRP and ply, the slab-sided effect being minimized by a rubbing strake which also strengthens the join. Should the extension be in GRP, a mould of some sort will have to be erected to lay it up against. Hardboard liberally coated with a release agent will give fairly good curves, but as the results are unlikely to be up to the standard of the hull, as regards finish, much rubbing down, filling and painting is usually necessary.

Superstructure design should be taken very seriously, and should embrace all factors both above and below decks. Observation of other boats' design and scantlings will help to produce a strong and serviceable result. Should you feel that this part of the project is beyond you, a sensible alternative is to arrange for a naval architect to do this part for you, perhaps in conjunction with your own ideas.

Whoever undertakes this job, drawings, or at least detailed diagrams are essential, in side, end and plan elevations. In this way many mistakes can be avoided and the end result will look as you intended.

Scantlings will have a direct effect on stability. The centre of gravity wants to be as low as possible so decks and deck beams should not be too heavy. A combination of strength and lightness is the goal. When making comparisons with other boats be sure that displacement is similar. If you have a light displacement cruising yacht hull, for example, don't be misled into taking your ideas from a traditional heavy displacement type, even where the overall length and beam are similar. A superstructure using scantlings for the latter would make your boat dangerously top-heavy and unseaworthy.

Sufficient strength can be obtained by design rather than the use of heavy material. It will be seen, for example, that cabin tops are, almost without exception, cambered into a shallow arch. Curves have provided strength in building of any kind for centuries. Even with the use of lightweight beams and thin ply, this shape gives great rigidity, and counters the tendency to depress under load. A flat top would require much heavier deck beams to achieve the same result.

Side decks, being much narrower, may be flat, but should be sloped gently down towards the gunwales. This will aid the clearance of water, and prevent puddles forming when the boat lies level which might encourage leaks or rot or both.

Construction

You (or the manufacturer) will have already braced the open hull to the correct beam and shape, using two or three temporary thwarts (crossbeams, usually about 4″ × 2″ in section, glassed in at the ends with small GRP brackets that can be chiselled off later), and glassed in the necessary stringers.

The next job is to fasten the beam shelf which will support the outer ends of the deck beams.

The shelf should be of good quality softwood such as Douglas fir or European larch, selected with as straight a grain as possible.

As the half joint notches to take the deck beam ends should be pre-cut, the easiest procedure is to clamp the shelf, in one piece or suitable sections, into place, all around the hull, using G-cramps. With any luck you can borrow some of these, because you probably won't need so many all at once again.

Now using a piece of timber the same width as the deck beams, and as long as the beam of the hull, mark off the position of each notch, making sure that the timber is always at right angles to the keel.

The shelf, or parts of, may now be removed and the halving joints cut. (Identify each piece to ensure accurate reassembly.) The notches should be cut out slightly undersize so that the deck beams are a good fit. It is always better to err on the small side with this part of the joint, because it is an easy matter to plane a few slivers off the other to achieve a fit.

Before the shelf is reassembled, it is a good idea to treat this (if you haven't done so already) and all other timber with a clear wood preservative to discourage future fungal attack. Obviously the wood will have to be allowed to dry thoroughly before fitting.

There are two ways of fitting the beam shelf to be dealt with here, both of which are adequate, and the method you choose largely depends on the size of the hull and the amount of 'bend' needed. Obviously, the thinner the timber the easier it will be to bend, so if the hull is large and the shelf quite thick, the second method may be easier.

The first way is to clamp the shelf back into position after the notches have been cut and the back has been contoured as necessary to fit the hull. The contouring may be achieved by bedding the shelf on to epoxy or polyester filler paste.

The next step is to drill through the hull and shelf every twelve to eighteen inches (or between each notch) and bolt the two together, using stainless steel bolts preferably, or good quality galvanized steel. Now, using the techniques already described, making suitable radii, the shelf should be glassed in, avoiding the notches.

It is normally best to use bolts with counter-sunk heads, which may be let in flush with the GRP hull, or even sunk beneath the surface and then filled with suitably coloured gel resin. The latter, however, is not often necessary because a wooden rubbing strake usually covers this area. It is worth mentioning at this point that it saves time to fit this rubbing strake now. Remove the bolts once the glass has set. Clamp the strake into position, drill through from the inside using the existing bolt holes, counter-sink the strake, re-fit the bolts and plug all the holes (*see* Fig. 9).

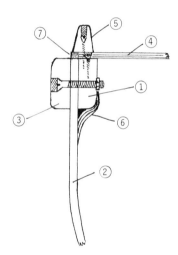

Fig. 9:   1. Beam shelf   2. Hull
3. Rubbing strake   4. Deck   5. Toe rail
6. CSM   7. Hardwood fillet to cover
ply end grain (glued and pinned)

Internally, the beam shelf will most often be covered by lining of some sort. In some cases though, maybe by personal choice, it will remain visible, and it is either because of this, or the bending problems of a thick shelf, that the next method may be more suitable.

Glass in a half thickness shelf, and then, using an epoxy adhesive, fasten the inner half by screwing, or through-bolting. The rubbing strake can also be fitted at this stage if desired, as in method one.

The notches, incidentally, need only be cut in the inner half of the shelf.

The next job is to fit the main bulkheads, i.e. those that go from keel to coachroof. It is here that you have the main advantage over those building from a complete shell; this is because it is much easier to shape and fit these large areas of ply when they can be lowered in from the top. They can also be clamped into position for glassing by hanging them from a beam laid athwart temporarily pinned to the beam shelf (*see* Fig. 10).

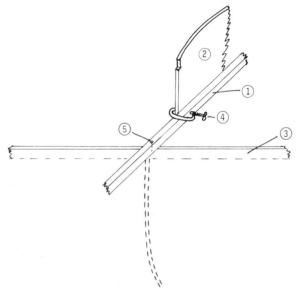

Fig. 10:   1. Beam   2. Bulkhead   3. Beam shelf   4. G-cramp   5. Temporary fastening

The main bulkheads are pre-cut to the exact shape of the deck, coachroof and coamings (*see* Fig. 11) and also notched for shelves, carlines and mast pad or fore and aft king plank where necessary. Limber holes are also cut at the lowest point.

Pre-cutting of doorways is also easier when you are still able to work horizontally, but some builders are against doing this because it can lead to distortion. A full-height doorway twenty or more inches wide will remove a fair amount of strength from a sheet of ply, and although a good measure of this will be replaced in the building process, it will need careful handling during installation.

With an electric jigsaw it is no great hardship to cut out a doorway *in situ*, and a plumb-line can be used to make sure of the vertical.

In either case, starting off with the forward bulkhead positioned by measuring as in Fig. 5, use a long straight-edge to check for distortion.

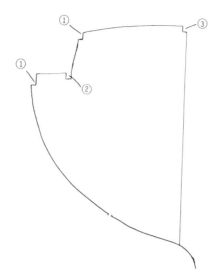

Fig. 11: Part bulkhead ready for fitting
1. Notches for beam shelves 2. Notch for carline 3. Notch for central fore and aft beam (when fitted)

Check from all angles, i.e. horizontal, vertical and diagonal, and make sure the edges meet all the marks on the hull.

I would like to dwell on these marks for a second; having marked the bulkhead position on the gunwales, lay a straight beam of wood or metal etc. across from mark to mark, and using a plumb-line, make more marks each side from the gunwale down to the keel (*see* Fig. 6).

Should there be any distortion, it can normally be taken out by glassing in small GRP brackets where the fit is good and then using suitable lengths of timber to brace the rest into shape until it is glassed in. Use pads of scrap ply between the brace and the bulkhead to avoid surface damage.

It is most important to get each bulkhead absolutely vertical and square with the keel centreline because this gives you the datum points for fitting all the furniture.

As both marine ply and exterior quality ply is very expensive, there is a lot to be said for using templates or formers. These can be fabricated from hardboard, and you only need enough to make up one half of the largest bulkhead. Any discrepancies or variations between one side of the hull and the other can be marked on the template, e.g. plus or minus so much, and marked with an arrow. This template can then be trimmed down for the next largest and so on.

Although sheets of ply normally come in 2440 mm × 1220 mm, the metric equivalent of 8′ × 4′, larger sizes are obtainable on special order, and still larger sizes can be made up by scarfing two sheets together. A more practical solution is usually to use standard width sheets in two or more sections (*see* Fig. 12). These can be arranged in whatever is the most convenient way. For example, two four-foot widths leaving a central two-foot gap for a doorway will span a ten-foot beam. If more than four feet is required in any one section, then two special five-foot width sheets may solve the problem, or a butt strap may be the answer (*see* Fig. 12) and the timber forming the strap can usually be incorporated as a door pillar.

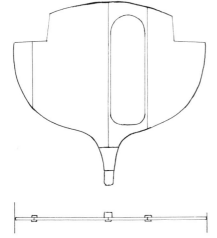

Fig. 12:   Sections of ply forming a full bulkhead. Joints are reinforced by hardwood trim and a central mast pillar. All glued and screwed

The length of eight feet will normally be sufficient for all but very deep-keel yachts, and here, a part bulkhead up to floor level will serve.

With all the bulkheads fully glassed in place, the temporary thwarts may be removed without fear of the hull distorting.

To save defacing the ply with resin runs, it is a good idea to mask off the area, except where the glass is going to be applied around the edges. Old newspapers held in place by ordinary masking tape will keep the bulkhead nice and clean.

A floor to stand on

Unless you are working on a flat-bottomed boat you will by this stage have had your fill of the knee-wearing frustration of trying to stop yourself and your tools from sliding down towards the keel. There is a lot to be said for working on a level surface.

To save any confusion, the floors on a traditional boat are the timbers tying two opposing frames to the keelson. In most small craft they also double as floor bearers. The part you will shortly be walking on is called the cabin sole.

Before installing the floors there are one or two points to consider.
Firstly, it is handy and safe to be able to reach all parts of the hull under the water-line, just in case you are ever unlucky enough to need to plug a hole temporarily.

Secondly, provision must be made for skin fittings under the cabin sole.

Thirdly, you may wish to have underfloor tanks or other stowage which must be planned for, and space must be available for piping and wiring.

Finally, the height of the floors must allow sufficient headroom.

The type of floors or bearers you use depends on the beam of the boat at floor height and the sort of tanks you decide on. I have a personal preference for the flexible type, because they can be removed for bilge inspection or access. These come in various shapes and sizes and if, for instance, you use the long, sausage type, they may lie athwart a fairly flat-bottomed motor cruiser, or longitudinally in the deeper, narrower bilge of a sailing boat. Accordingly, the floors in the former may be of the bulkhead type which divide the bilge into compartments, whereas in the latter case they will have to be of the joist type, allowing for a clear run underneath (*see* Figs. 13 & 14).

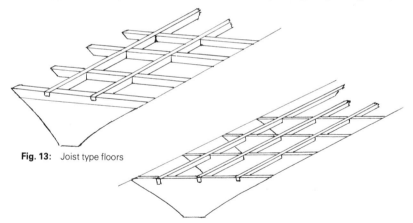

Fig. 13:   Joist type floors

Fig. 14:   Bulkhead type floors

In either case one of two systems will have to be used to provide access; these will be dealt with shortly.

In both cases the first job is to fit the floors, bearing in mind that the cabin sole, if not to flex, must be supported every sixteen to eighteen inches. Longitudinal stringers should also be added to support the fore and aft edges of the hatches.

It will be seen from Figures 13 & 14 that this is a simple matter of making notches in the bulkhead type or halving joints in the joist type.

The main thing is to get each section level and horizontal. In the case of a cabin with a main bulkhead at either end, a floor bearer should be attached to each at the desired height up from the keel. The procedure will be to fit one, making sure that it is completely level, then with the use of a straight-edge which reaches from one end of the cabin to the other, and a spirit-level resting on the straight-edge, the height of the opposite bearer can be determined and marked. When using a spirit-level, always test it in both directions. For some unaccountable reason they do not always give the same reading when reversed 180 degrees. It obviously pays to carry out this test in the shop at the time of purchase, but if you didn't you will either have to take a mean average between the two readings, or buy a better one. The long, aluminium, builders' type are the best, but a short one will also be necessary for areas of limited space.

These end bearers need usually only be a batten of two or maybe three by one (inches) and will eventually be screwed and glued to the bulkhead. For the time being, however, just screw them into place until the position of the longitudinals has been determined, at which time they may be removed to have the notches cut.

With the level-bearer at each end, the batten you are using for a straight-edge may be utilized to give you the exact height of each floor to be built in-between.

As weight low down is normally desirable, except maybe in the case of ultra lightweight multihulls, there is no harm in using good, stout timber for the floors to give a nice, solid feel to the cabin sole. The bulkhead type can often be made up from heavy ply offcuts from the main bulkheads. They do not necessarily need to be in one piece either, because there is no objection to glassing them right up to cabin sole level from each side, thus making the ply merely the core of a fibreglass sandwich. This method will avoid saturation of the ply should the bilges ever flood.

When touching on the subject of bilge-water, limber holes should be cut into each bulkhead where it crosses the lowest point over the keel, to allow any accumulation of water to drain back into the well or sump for pumping out. If two or three inches of plastic hose are put through the limber hole so that it protrudes either side (*see* Fig. 15) and then glassed in, water passing through it will be unable to get at the vulnerable end grain of the ply. The pipe should be of at least one-inch bore, or alternatively, two-inch bore pipe can be cut in half and inserted as an inverted 'U' section. The latter method has the advantage of allowing the last drops of bilge-water through.

The ply floors may be easily measured by moving the end-to-end straight-edge from one side of the hull to the other in six-inch stages, keeping it parallel to the fore and aft centreline and measuring vertically downwards to the hull at each stage. When each floor has

Fig. 15: 1. Limber holes 2. Bulkhead

been cut out and located in position, check that it is parallel to the main bulkhead, and use the straight-edge to make sure it is the right height from one side of the boat to the other. If it is too high, cut wood off the bottom, where it touches the hull, rather than spoil the top edge, which should be nice and straight. If, on the other hand, it fails to reach the straight-edge, there is no problem. Cut another straight-edge from a spare batten (selecting it for straightness), hang the ply floor by temporary screws (*see* Fig. 16), fill the discrepancy with filler paste, making the usual radius, and glass in place.

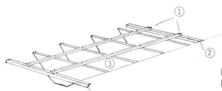

Fig. 16: 1. Battens resting on (2) 2. Ledges fastened to bulkheads at each end of the compartment 3. Bulkhead type floor

With all the floors glassed in, the end-to-end stringers may be cut (the straight-edge battens may well do here), layed in the desired positions and marked. Notches may be cut *in situ* in the floors, but the end bearers can now be removed, the notches cut, and then screwed and glued back permanently in place.

The same sort of system may be used for the joist type floors, i.e. cut slightly undersize, hang from the straight-edge battens by screws or clamps, fill any gaps, and glass in place. In deep hulls, where the end of the joist may meet the hull abruptly, it is important to spread the load as much as possible either by glassing in two or three layers of mat into a pad at the point of contact, or by placing a plywood pad at each end for the joist to rest on and then glassing in the whole. This will prevent distortion or high spots appearing in the hull. Ply pads should be bedded down on filler to be solid against the hull.

Access hatches

As mentioned previously, one of two systems may be used. The first is to fasten permanently a plywood cabin sole to the floors and stringers (paint the underside first for protection against damp and rot), having first cut out strategically placed access holes. The cut-outs will form the actual hatch, and will have been cut down the centreline of the floor and stringer so that the latter forms a lip on which the hatch can rest (*see* Figs. 17 & 17a).

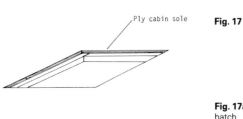

Ply cabin sole

Fig. 17

Fig. 17a: 1. Cabin sole   2. Access hatch   3. Finger hole   4. Support battens (bolted if walked upon, glued to cabin sole)

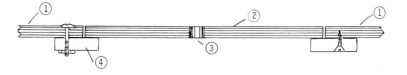

With this system the cabin sole can be laid straight away, provided the hatches are placed carefully so they will not interfere with the future built-in furniture, or have their function prohibited by it.

The second system is to treat the whole cabin sole as lift-up sections, apart from those areas that would be covered by furniture.

In both cases access hatches should be provided under the furniture unless these areas can be easily reached from an adjacent hatch.

Lift hooks are available that fold flat into the cabin sole when not in use, but one-inch finger holes are just as handy.

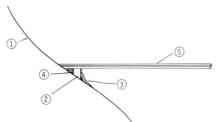

Fig. 18: 1. Hull   2. Timber ledge   3. CSM   4. Filler   5. Cabin sole

Where the cabin sole meets the hull at the sides, it may be necessary to glass in a ledge for it to rest on; make sure this is filled so as not to become a water trap (*see* Fig. 18).

To give the access hatch a greater area to rest on where ply floors are being used, a batten of around 2″ × 1″ may be screwed and glued along one or both sides of the top edge (*see* Fig. 19). To make sure the end grain is protected, seal it well with paint, or polyester resin. It is best not to glass over the top as it is almost impossible to do this without leaving ridges which will make the cabin sole sit unevenly. Some builders make these bulkhead-type floors half an inch or so under height and then put a capping on by gluing and pinning.

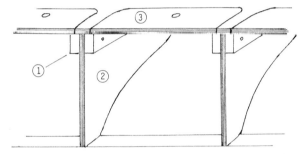

Fig. 19: 1. 2″ × 1″ batten   2. Bulkhead type floor   3. Access hatch with finger hole

Carlines and deck beams

The carlines are the longitudinal lengths of timber that run approximately parallel to the beam shelf and provide support for the inboard ends of the side deck beams. They normally run from the aft foredeck beam back to wherever the side decks end.

They may be made from a good softwood such as Douglas fir or spruce, both of which are quite easy to plane and drill, and also glue well.

Select straight grained lengths if possible so that curves remain constant.

The deck beams are traditionally made from hardwood such as the African redwood that passes for mahogany these days.

The first step will be to make and fasten the full-width deck beams i.e. the foredeck, the bridge deck (if any) and the aft deck.

To take a fairly conventional design, the first deck beam (starting from the bow) may well be incorporated with a small bulkhead forming the chain locker, and after this, depending on the size of the boat, there will be perhaps three or four full-width deck beams before the coachroof.

The design will probably call for these to be curved to form the camber we have already spoken of, but as this may well be milder than that of the coachroof it may not be necessary to laminate these beams, but merely to cut or plane the shape out of solid timber (*see* Fig. 20).

Should lamination be necessary the technique will be the same as for coachroof beams to be discussed shortly.

As the foredeck is often subject to a lot of strain due to anchor winches, cleats or maybe even a mast in smaller boats, a central support called the king plank is let in to the crown of the deck beams (*see* Fig. 21).

Fig. 20

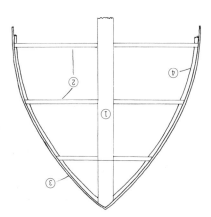

Fig. 21: 1. King plank   2. Deck beams   3. Hull   4. Beam shelf

There may also be space for a forward hatch in-between the anchor winch and the front of the cabin. Apart from its more normal uses for passing sail bags or other gear up or down, a forward hatch is a great safety feature, giving another exit point in cases of fire or sinking. Bearing this in mind, the hatch should be large enough to allow an adult person rapid access. Some of the cheaper ready-made hatches on the market would hamper the progress of a lean pigmy. Siting the hatch on the foredeck has the advantage of giving a step up in the form of one or both of the forward berths, which normally makes it easy to scrabble through the rest of the way. There is a tendency in some designs to site this hatch in the forward end of the coachroof above the head and shower compartment. This is great for ventilation, but unless you are a trained gymnast you will need to provide steps up to it.

The space between two beams will normally be enough to allow for a hatch (*see* Fig. 22), but where the design calls for lightweight beams close together, at least one beam will have to butt up to the hatch coaming.

Once again, make the deck beams marginally wider than the notches in the beam shelf. An exact fit is the aim, and a few slivers shaved off the ends will usually ensure this.

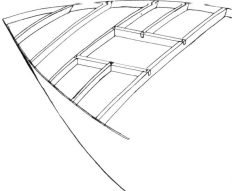

Fig. 22:   Arrangement for forward hatch in foredeck

The curvature of each beam must be the same, so it is as well to work from a hardboard template of the longest. As the boat tapers towards the bow or stern, the others will be the same shape from the centre or crown of the template out to where they meet the beam shelf.

With each beam in place, check the fore and aft run with a batten, making sure there are no dips or high spots that would distort the decking when laid. They should be fairly true if they were cut with the same curve as the template, but it is not difficult to cut too much or too little depth in the halving joint tongue, especially as it meets the beam shelf at an angle as the bow curves inwards.

Correction may be made by cutting a little more off the tongue until it fits down level with the beam shelf, or by packing it up with an additional piece of wood glued into place.

Before finally fastening and gluing the beams into position, cut all necessary notches for the hatch or king plank while they can be removed and worked on in comfort.

Halving joints are among the simplest to make, but still require care. It is easy to make a mistake by being in too much of a hurry, but the most common cause of errors is not having the timber firmly clamped while you are working on it. Laying the piece on a bench or trestle or dining-room chair and trying to hold it down with a hand and a foot whilst at the same time trying to cut it with the other hand is asking for trouble. I speak here from bitter experience of far too long a time trying, but only seldom achieving a good fit. The answer used to be laborious use of vices and clamps, but things have now been greatly simplified by the introduction of the Black and Decker Workmate. Here is a portable bench that allows you to work in a fairly dignified position and use both hands for cutting and chiselling.

More on tools later. Now for the side deck beams.

These will slope upwards towards the centre at the same angle as the last full-width deck beam. In fact, if they were not to be interrupted by the coachroof or cabin, they would be the same shape. As they will probably only be a foot or eighteen inches in length, however, they should be as near straight as makes no difference.

If your cabin sides are going to be straight, the beams may all be different lengths, depending on the shape of the hull. Some designs call for the cabin sides to follow the curve of the hull and run parallel to the gunwale, in which case the beams will be the same length. In either case the inboard end terminates at the carline and is notched into it.

The notches for the carlines are already cut into the bulkheads, the aft foredeck beam and the next full-width deck beam aft, which could be the bridge deck or aft deck beam (in some designs a bulkhead forms the last side deck beam at each end and this is where the carlines terminate).

In either case it helps to lay the carlines in position, firstly to mark out the length of each beam and secondly to mark where each notch is to be cut.

Where the carline is curved, check that the curve is equal on both port and starboard and if necessary 'spring' into place by drawing it towards the side with a sash cramp or forcing it away with a prop or two.

Each side deck beam should be in line with its opposite number; a good way to ensure this is to use a straight-edge batten the same width as the beams that reaches from one side to the other. When this is in line with each opposite notch in the beam shelf a mark can be made where it crosses each carline.

When all the marks are made and the deck beams cut with a tongue at each end, the carlines may be removed for the notches to be cut.

This may sound a laborious process, but bear in mind that few of these joints will be at right angles to each other, so only marking *in situ* will ensure accuracy.

Laminating deck and coachroof beams

Where there is to be a considerable curve in a beam it would be too wasteful to cut it out of solid timber, and steam bending can be a complicated process. However, with the introduction of modern resorcinol glues, laminating thin strips together provides the ideal solution. Strong, light and very little wastage of wood.

Laminating is accepted boat building practice, indeed, where yards are still making wooden hulls it is quite normal for stems, stern-posts, frames, keels and dead-woods to be laminated. The only proviso is that the work is done in the right conditions, i.e. warm and dry, which for amateur boat-builders often means the front room, much to the interest, amazement or disgust of other inhabitants.

The glue must be of good quality and used according to the makers instructions, and finally, the work must be clamped up really tight during the whole of the curing period.

Wood to be laminated should be of an easily bendable thickness, half an inch or maybe less, and a former should be made up to ensure that each beam is identical (*see* Fig. 23).

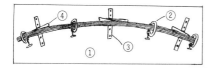

Fig. 23: 1. Former – ply or plank, polythene-covered to prevent beam sticking 2. G-cramps 3. 4" × 2" blocks bolted to former 4. Hardwood wedges

To speed up the process, it is quite acceptable to make up wide beams and slice them down to the required size after curing. In this way two or three may be made up in one gluing.

Be generous with the glue, it should cover the entire area to be bonded, leaving no voids. The surplus that is squeezed out as the clamps are tightened can be wiped off with a damp cloth, and the beam may be sanded clean later.

As when using all adhesives, make sure the wood is clean, dry and free from grease or dust.

When cutting the strips to form the beams, remember that bending will decrease the overall length, so allow extra to compensate. End joints and other areas to cut away for mast pads etc. may be done after curing.

Short beams that are interrupted by hatch coamings should be made up on the relevant part of the former so they are the same shape as the others. This will avoid the wastage of making up a whole beam and then cutting out the area for the hatch.

Laying the deck

The deck may be laid in one or two layers. In most cases a single thickness is easiest, usually about half an inch (or the metric equivalent, twelve millimetres) for larger boats around ten metres, and three-eighths (six millimetres) for smaller craft; however, different designs call for different scantlings, so this should be checked.

Two layers are usually only necessary on the main deck where a decorative facing is to be used, such as sheets of imitation teak decking, or even teak or iroko (similar but cheaper) strips for laying the real thing. In this case, to save the risk of becoming top heavy, both layers should be of half the designed thickness.

Where the beams do not run true it will be virtually impossible to avoid air gaps or voids in-between the two layers, which is why the beams must be made true.

To save wasting ply it is once again a good idea to make up templates of hardboard or cardboard, especially for the bow section. As in the case of the bulkheads it is really only necessary to make up one for one side of the foredeck, as this, turned over, should be near enough the shape of the other side.

Aim for a neat centreline join between the bow and the centre of the coachroof and cut the rest a little oversize, because any that projects over the side of the boat can be easily planed off flush. If this is impossible because of the rubbing strake or raised gunwale section, then it is safer to use templates all round to ensure a good fit.

All joins should be made to coincide with deck beams, each piece terminating at the beam's centreline. Once again, be generous with the glue. Use either brass screws or barb-ring nails for fastening, but make sure each goes home tightly. In cases where the beams are going to be a feature below, don't forget to go below after fastening each section to wipe of the surplus glue with a damp cloth.

Coachroof coamings

You now have a decked hull with only the main bulkheads protruding above deck level, and these form the shape of the coachroof and coamings.

The rear main bulkhead usually forms the division between cabin and cockpit, so this is where the coachroof will end. The coamings, or cabin sides may also end here, or they may merely dip down and run aft to the rear of the cockpit. Once again it depends on the design. In any case it is unlikely that the whole length could be cut out of one sheet of ply, so for the object of this exercise we will presume that it ends at the bulkhead and that any extension into the cockpit area will be joined on later.

The next thing to fit will be the coaming piece. This may be made from the same material as the carlines, i.e. Douglas fir, European larch etc., and should be at least an inch and a half wider so that when fastened on edge to the latter it projects an inch or so above deck level (*see* Fig. 24). This provides a fastening point for the bottom edge of the side coamings in-between each bulkhead.

A similar piece is fitted to the aft face of the aft foredeck beam for the front coaming, and this may be upright or angled back in accordance with the design (*see* Fig. 25).

In some cases the front piece may be mounted on the deck, as in designs where it is curved or 'V'd' but unfortunately there is no room to cover every design here; the essence is to provide a mounting point.

The front coaming is not that simple a shape, as it is curved at the bottom to fit the deck and will very likely have a steeper curve along the top edge to fit the coachroof (this will normally be more steeply arched to gain internal headroom). So once more, a template is advisable.

Where the front coaming is to be angled aft, the top and bottom edges will also need angling (*see* Fig. 26).

As this front coaming may have to bear the brunt of rough seas, owners of sea-going craft often, wisely, do without a portlight or window, but for those intending to use calm water it is sometimes difficult to cut holes in this area after fitting.

It will be necessary to attach a beam to the inside top edge of the front coaming for the front of the coachroof to be fastened to, and it is

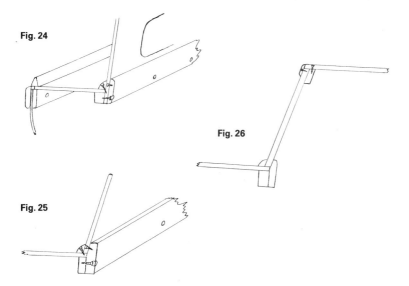

Fig. 24

Fig. 26

Fig. 25

often simpler to cut this one out of solid timber. If the front is to be raked you may find it easier to leave a suitable amount projecting upwards, and plane it off to the right angle after the side coamings have been attached.

With the beam glued and screwed in place and a pillar of quadrant beading fastened in each corner (*see* Fig. 27) the front can now be fitted.

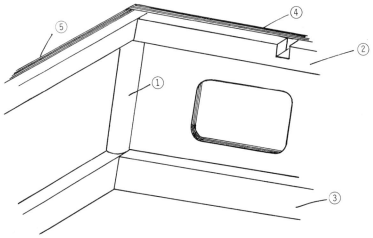

Fig. 27:   1. Quadrant beading or square section with free corner rounded off   2. Coachroof beam shelf   3. Coaming piece   4. Side coaming   5. Front coaming

There are now definite boundaries for the side coamings, so they may be cut out and any window apertures made.

Before fitting the sides it must be noted that a good fastening cannot be made into the end grain of ply, so bearing this in mind, the main bulkheads need similar treatment to the front coaming (*see* Fig. 28).

Along the top edge of the side coamings it will be necessary to fit a shelf that performs the same function as the beam shelf, i.e. a fastening point for the ends of the coachroof beams (*see* Fig. 29). There should be a cut-out in the top corner of the central bulkheads for the shelf to pass through (*see* Fig. 11), although on the aft bulkhead it can rest in a slot cut into the upright you have just fastened (*see* Fig. 30).

Now the side coamings may be fitted.

It is worth mentioning that if the coamings have much of a curve fore and aft, it will probably be easier to spring them into place, and fasten the shelf afterwards, if necessary by laminating it in thin strips as for the beams. Also, if there is a pronounced inboard rake, leave enough of the shelf sticking out above the ply of the coaming so that

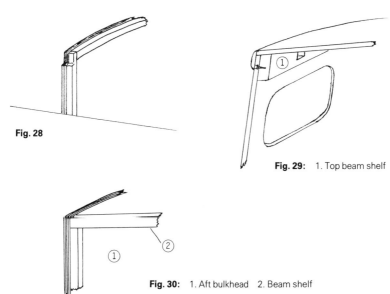

Fig. 28

Fig. 29:   1. Top beam shelf

Fig. 30:   1. Aft bulkhead   2. Beam shelf

you can plane it to the right angle to take the decking, i.e. the same angle as the coachroof beams.

The coachroof will most probably have a sliding hatch at the cockpit end and possibly a forward hatch as well, if the latter hasn't already been built into the foredeck.

Depending on the frequency of the beams, this may or may not mean any interrupted lengths (*see* Fig. 31).

As for the foredeck beams, it is of paramount importance to get all the coachroof beams level with each other and the bulkheads. To make sure of this, lay a fore and aft straight-edge batten, moving it from one side to the other a few inches at a time to check for high and low spots. Any discrepancies should be cured at this stage by sanding or planing down high spots, raising the beam slightly in its notch where it may be low, or in drastic cases even adding a thin lamination to the beam.

It is worth spending time on this to ensure a smooth, strong and creak-free cabin top. This is especially so where a steeply cambered coachroof is concerned because it will be easier to lay the deck in layers.

Now the deck can be laid, using templates to cut the ply in the same manner as the foredeck. Any joins should always be along the centreline of a beam, or a fore and aft plank if there is one. The hatch areas may be cut out before or after laying the deck, whichever is easier. Once again, be generous with the glue, especially where two

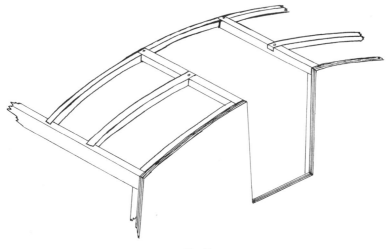

Fig. 31

layers of ply are involved and in this case apply the fastenings in a sequence to squeeze out excess glue, i.e. from the centre outwards.

In warm weather, when the glue is liable to set quicker, a certain amount of speed will be necessary. Barb-ring nails are probably the speediest to apply, but if you are using brass screws make sure all the holes are pre-drilled and countersunk. A pump-type screwdriver is quite fast, as is a screwdriver bit in a brace. I have found a screwdriver bit in an electric drill very effective, although I am sure the manufacturers wouldn't recommend it, especially as screwdriver attachments are available. The problem with this sort of attachment being that unless you intend decking a lot of boats, its use will be very infrequent.

If you are using barb-ring nails, remember that once the ply covers the beams you will no longer be able to see where they are. It helps a lot to have all the fastening points marked out first, or at least lines denoting all the beam centrelines. Otherwise, especially if you are in a hurry, it is surprisingly easy to miss a beam altogether.

Despite the extra expense, use BS 1088 marine grade ply for all external use such as decks and coamings, and before laying any sort of covering treat all the bare surfaces, especially the end grain, with wood preservative.

After one or two coats of this has thoroughly dried off, the deck covering of your choice may be laid as per the maker's instructions, taken over the edge of the coachroof or deck, and battening may be applied as in Fig. 32 to tidy up all the edges, and beading for the corners. It will almost certainly be necessary in some if not all cases to

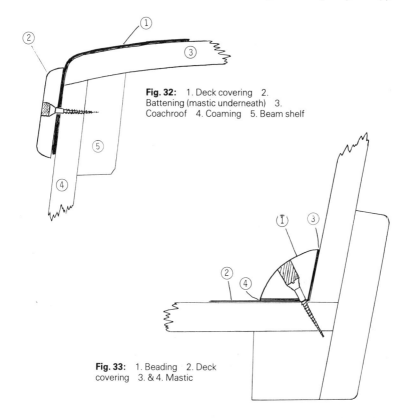

Fig. 32: 1. Deck covering 2. Battening (mastic underneath) 3. Coachroof 4. Coaming 5. Beam shelf

Fig. 33: 1. Beading 2. Deck covering 3. & 4. Mastic

alter the angle of the quadrant beading by planing the underside (*see* Fig. 33). Use a generous quantity of mastic in both cases to ensure a watertight seal.

Aft cabins

Apart from the fact that it will usually be considerably shorter than the main cabin, an aft cabin may be built in exactly the same way. The bulkhead which forms the rear of the cockpit area will be the front end of this cabin, and it may well be cut away under deck level, where this is allowed by tankage and engine space, to allow leg room in the berths.

When this is done, these areas will always be boxed in to seal them off from the engine room. Often as little as six inches of extended space can make all the difference between a comfortable or cramped berth.

Cockpits

The cockpit, whether aft or centre, may be treated like a cabin without a roof.

Normally the coamings will be only about half the height, and may dip down in a curve, or sheer, from the coachroof until they level out a foot or two aft. Where ply is used, a shelf and capping will be necessary both to protect the end grain and provide a slightly less painful surface on which to sit.

In aft cockpit boats Samson-posts may be usefully incorporated into each corner for effective mooring points (*see* Fig. 34). They are so much more practical than the yachty little cleats currently available that tend to get choked up by more than a couple of turns of decent sized rope.

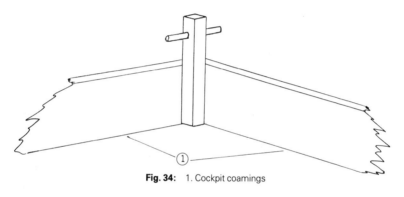

Fig. 34: 1. Cockpit coamings

There has always been a lot of controversy over whether or not a cockpit should be self-draining. It very much depends on the usage, but there is no doubt that if a boat with a large aft cockpit were to become flooded, the trim of the boat may be upset beyond the point of no return, and cause it to disappear beneath the waves stern first. If, on the other hand, that water were allowed to run through the entire length of the boat, it may well stay afloat long enough for action to be taken.

Although we are talking about extreme conditions it is possible to be caught out through bad luck or bad planning. Once, when through a mixture of the latter and a fair measure of foolhardiness, I was caught in gale conditions in the English Channel some thirty miles offshore in a thirty-one-foot motor boat with a very large cockpit and most of the weight concentrated in two inboard/outboard diesels on the stern (which mercifully kept running half under water), we were swamped by a particularly evil wave which flooded the boat to some six inches above the saloon floor level. During the violent activity that followed, pumping and baling, the boat was actually more stable in the very rough seas than she had been before. The bilge-water was acting as ballast. I might add that this was not very comforting at the time, but nevertheless, I am inclined to think that the same amount of water contained in the cockpit would have been disastrous.

My own thoughts are that large cockpits, if they are to be self-draining, should be made quite shallow, have large and effective drains with non-return flaps, and have decent sized benches for sitting on (which can also double as extra berths with a cockpit cover). In this way, not too much water is allowed to accumulate from a swamping, and it can be evacuated quickly.

The cockpit sole may have to be made removable for access to the engine compartment, or indeed, for removal of the engine if need be. In a steel boat, a steel hatch would stay in place when flooded, but a wooden one would tend to float up to the surface and allow the water through. For the cockpit to be self-draining, therefore, a wooden hatch must be held in place by mechanical means such as spring clips, nuts and bolts, or sliding bolts etc.

The cockpit sole must naturally clear the top of the engine, so this height must be known in advance, otherwise this part of the job will have to be left until the engine is installed.

Under the side decks there is useful locker space for ropes, fenders etc., or perhaps, on one side, a pilot berth in from the saloon (*see* Fig. 45c).

Bearers for the cockpit sole should, like those for the cabin sole, be strong enough to give a nice, solid feel underfoot. Any bearers that cover the engine will have to be made removable. One good design I saw recently used a 'U' section steel channel under loose boards (*see* Fig. 35). This meant that any rain-water trickled down in-between the boards into the channel which incorporated two drainage holes connected to skin fittings in the hull by plastic piping.

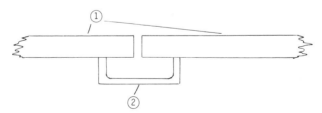

Fig. 35:   1. Cockpit sole   2. 'U' section channel

Whilst making no claim to being self-draining under swamping conditions, this design kept the bilge dry even under heavy rainfall—a pertinent point when you consider that rain-water has been responsible for sinking any number of unattended boats at their moorings.

Hatches

Your choice of hatch depends, to a great extent, on both usage and the amount you want to spend.

There are many good ready-made hatches available, quite a few of which are large enough to climb through, watertight and strong. If you intend using a ready-made hatch you only have to make the right size of aperture so that it may be screwed or bolted down, and bedded on the rubber seals provided, or on a suitable mastic.

The advantage of the ready-made hatch is that it is usually transparent, and so performs the function of skylight as well. Reputable makes can also be stomped on by all but stiletto heels without risk of damage.

They are also expensive.

Cheaper versions are obtainable, such as the caravan type, which have few of the above qualities but should keep out the rain; these can be suitable for static house-boats and some inland cruisers where getting out of trouble in a storm merely means tying up well and going in out of the rain.

It is not difficult to build your own hatches from mahogany and ply. The hatch coamings should be screwed and glued to the inside of the aperture formed by the deck beams and longitudinal beams. They should preferably be of mahogany if the corners are to be butted (*see* Fig. 36) because the exposed end grain is not so vulnerable as ply. They should protrude above the deck level three or four inches. The athwart coamings should be arched. Now a lid should be made up (*see* Fig. 37) with the same degree of arch, and the internal measurement half an inch to an inch greater than the coamings. The lid is hinged from pads on the deck (*see* Fig. 38) so that when tightly shut forms a good fit with the coamings. Sliding bolts on the inside of the lid keep it secure against natural disasters or inquisitive humans (*see* Fig. 39).

Although hinged hatches are used for the main companion-way from the cockpit to the saloon, sliding hatches are more popular here unless there is a windscreen or some other obstacle.

The aperture for this hatch is normally from the aft main bulkhead to the next deck beam (*see* Fig. 31).

The coamings in this case are grooved, and about twice the length of the aperture so that the hatch may be slid right back and leave the maximum opening. It is most important for the coamings to be parallel. A lip is fitted in-between the two coamings above the deck beam to keep out any water that might be running in this direction (*see* Fig. 40).

The hatch may now be treated rather like an inverted kitchen drawer, because the principle is the same (*see* Fig. 41).

Nylon channel currently available from DIY stores may profitably

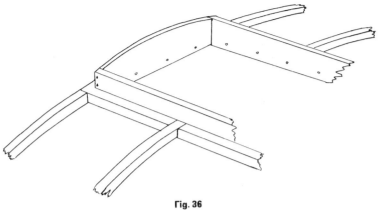

Fig. 36

(A)

Fig. 37a: 1. ¼" ply 2. ¼" teak planks glued to ply 3. Seams all caulked 4. Edge beading to cover end grain glued and pinned

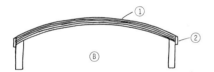

(B)

Fig. 37b: 1. ½" ply or 2" × ¼" ply 2. Edge beading

Fig. 38: 1. Hatch 2. Pad 3. Hinge

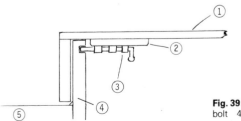

Fig. 39: 1. Hatch 2. Pad 3. Sliding bolt 4. Hatch coaming 5. Deck

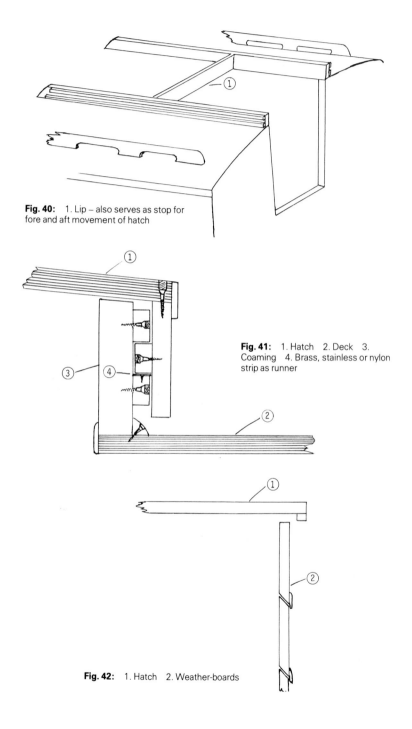

Fig. 40: 1. Lip – also serves as stop for fore and aft movement of hatch

Fig. 41: 1. Hatch 2. Deck 3. Coaming 4. Brass, stainless or nylon strip as runner

Fig. 42: 1. Hatch 2. Weather-boards

be stuck into the grooves (rough up the back and use epoxy adhesive) to ensure smooth running.

The aft end of the hatch should be made to overlap the door or weather-boards to keep out rain (*see* Fig. 42).

Both these hatches, hinged and sliding, are simple, basic but adequate designs which have served me well in the past. There are many others that are more elaborate, the designs of which appear in practical boat magazines from time to time.

Windscreens and wheelhouses

A windscreen is perhaps the simplest type of shelter, and may be purchased ready-made, with Perspex or safety glass in aluminium channel, ready to bolt on, or in the form of a canvas dodger with transparent panels in the front. It is also possible to have a combination of both.

Home-built versions are quite easy to make using sections of ply with window cut-outs. These must be fastened to a suitably raked moulding which is fastened through the deck, and the arrangement of the panels should make the screen self-supporting (*see* Fig. 43), although a central pillar does no harm.

A wheelhouse is normally totally enclosed, and therefore quite elaborate, but with the superstructure design method we have used, it would be quite a simple matter to build one into a centre cockpit

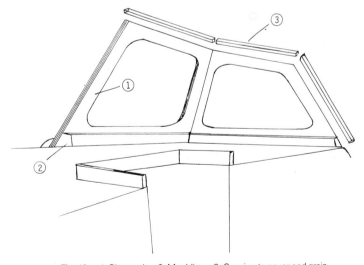

Fig. 43: 1. Ply panels   2. Moulding   3. Capping to cover end grain

version using exactly the same principle. The sides would merely be coamings extended upwards to the desired height, with a doorway cut into one or both sides. Above deck level it would become an integral part of the windscreen (just mentioned) at the front, and an extended bulkhead from the front of the rear cabin would form the back. The roof would be fastened in the same manner as the coachroof.

Where there was no aft cabin, the wheelhouse may either be left open to the cockpit, or have a bulkhead right across containing one or more doors. In this event, doors will not be needed in the sides.

Deck coverings

If you have made your own deck and superstructure, the horizontal surfaces will need protection from wear and the elements.

Deck paint is the simplest answer, and reference to a marine paint manufacturer will reveal types and method of application. This will nearly always involve priming and undercoating, but due to constant research this industry is bringing out new products regularly, so suffice it to say that the manufacturer's instructions should always be followed carefully.

Canvas is still used, but tends to be vulnerable to sharp footwear. However, properly laid and well painted it is quite non-slip.

Diamond pattern cork compound type decking is very tough, non-slip and attractive, even if it is rather hard on bare feet.

The types are numerous, as the advertisements will show, and some a lot more expensive than others. Some, like the latter, are thick enough and stiff enough to hold themselves down at the corners, if stuck properly. Others need tucking under corner beading or battens (*see* Fig. 32) to protect the edges.

In all cases it is of paramount importance to follow the sticking procedure assiduously, spreading the adhesive evenly and thoroughly, and laying the material in such a way as to eliminate trapped air bubbles, usually working from the centre outwards. Any parts that don't stick properly are an ideal place for rot to start.

Glassfibre sheathing offers good protection, and if applied well, i.e. on dry, keyed, grease-free timber, and rolled in really thoroughly, will add to the overall strength. Woven rovings and surface tissue make a good sheathing, and may be rubbed down and painted successfully.

GRP superstructures often have non-slip surfaces moulded in, but if not, coverage or patches of cork compound decking may be applied.

5 · The interior

The interior carpentry in a boat depends to some extent on its construction, the material it is made from and the use to which it will be put.

Theoretically, the build-in furniture of an inland cruiser need be no different to that of a touring caravan; it can, however, be stronger as weight will not be much of a problem. The idea is the same, to make maximum use of a small area.

Apart from the rectangular section of a barge or canal narrow boat, the main difference is the shape. Very few boats hold a straight line for any appreciable distance. The vast majority, in fact, are curved in all directions. For this reason it is rarely possible to use ready-made furniture unless the boat is very large. In small boats everything has to be built in, and attached in one way or another by bolting or bonding to the hull.

In GRP boats this has a bonus in providing extra strength in many areas, and adding to the overall stiffness. A good instance is the deck. A notorious area for this to flex, whether a GRP or ply superstructure, is the side decks in the saloon area, where there is a long distance in-between bulkheads. This can be completely cured by glassing in small bulkheads (see Fig. 44) which form the division between shelves and cupboards. Apart from the mast support, therefore, there is no need to add heavy reinforcement below decks, furniture of one sort or another, if bonded in properly, will do the job merely by becoming an integral part.

I doubt if the boat has yet been made that doesn't have a minute degree of flexibility in a rough sea, but the aim must be to keep it minimal. Any appreciable amount of movement could have disastrous effects. At the best, doors become distorted and refuse to open and close properly, and at the worst, bulkheads and internal structures can be torn away from the skin. The latter doesn't only apply to sea-going boats. Estuary and inland cruisers have known to 'dry out' at odd

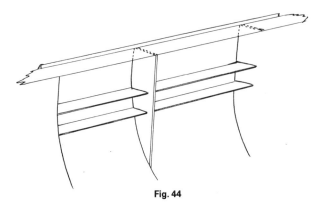

Fig. 44

angles imposing severe strains and stresses. Although this should not generally affect a strongly made boat, it could sound the death knell for a weak one.

Layout and accommodation

The main compartments of a boat are governed by the positions of the main bulkheads, and as we have previously mentioned, positioning the latter is often bound by mast support etc.

In boats over about twenty-four feet, however, there should still be some scope for personal choice modifications (*see* Fig. 45, A, B, C & D). For example, if you intend living aboard for long periods, a large, well designed galley is probably more practical than an extra berth. Again, you may be prepared to sacrifice a few inches of headroom to gain more underfloor tank space. A gain in one direction usually means a loss in another, but if it suits you personally, then the only other consideration is not being so extreme as to ruin the re-sale potential of the boat.

When planning your layout, therefore, it is worth spending time considering the pros and cons of each scheme, to find out whether or not it is practical. For instance, it is necessary to remember, when looking at a plan view, that the hull will probably be considerably narrower at floor level than it is at the gunwales. For this reason, cupboards that would appear to have ample stowage space on the drawing may have little practical use lower down. The same applies to berths, especially in the forward section of many boats, where the theoretical bed space might look palatial in a gunwale height plan, but may turn out to be almost inadequate when moved down two or three feet to make access feasible. This part of the boat often becomes shorter as well as narrower as you come down from the deck level.

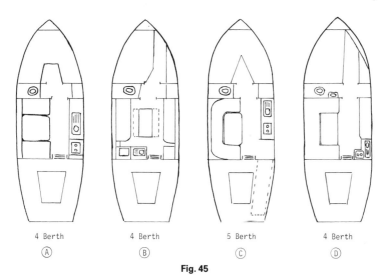

| 4 Berth | 4 Berth | 5 Berth | 4 Berth |
| Ⓐ | Ⓑ | Ⓒ | Ⓓ |

Fig. 45

Often the best and safest course is to keep the layout in the form of suggested sketches until the bulkheads are in, after which time you will have a much better idea of the possibilities.

Provided you have given thought to the future positioning of pipes, wiring and deck fittings, the order of fitting out is fairly flexible and may be governed by whim or situation. If you are living aboard, or intend to as soon as possible, priorities will include a galley, toilet compartment and somewhere to sit and sleep. I speak here from the spartan experience of a mattress laid on planks across the bilge, a toilet without a compartment necessitating those present to go outside (sometimes in the rain) if someone wanted to use it, a plastic jerrycan for water and a Primus stove. Needs must etc., but the point is that many things will have to be makeshift or temporary until time allows them to be done properly.

If there is no desperation other than your impatience to get afloat and sailing, it is usually better to build upwards from the cabin sole and thereby have some sort of comfort as you go. In this case a suitable order might be as follows: saloon benches, engine box or steps down into saloon (which might be one and the same), forward berths, after-cabin berths (if applicable), galley working surfaces and cupboards underneath, toilet, various cupboards and shelves, coachroof lining and window trim (after pre-positioning wire for lighting etc.) and so on.

Some of this work may be governed by the availability of materials, not to mention cash, access to equipment, and the fact that you might not be a very experienced carpenter.

Bearing this last point in mind, start with just the basic structures and leave the facings and fiddling bits until later, you will find that you improve enormously with practice, so you can make everything look pretty later on.

When the fundamental items are in place, lesser features such as bookshelves, glass and crockery holders may be built in the places most convenient for them, and this may not necessarily be where you originally planned to have them.

As a final note, take care to leave installation space for chain plates, winch and cleat pads etc.

Saloons

The most common fault with saloon benches built by home builders is the height. Even when care is taken to achieve a comfortable sitting position it is easy to forget the upholstery. The addition of a four- or five-inch cushion may leave short legs dangling. A total height of eighteen inches including the cushion is not unreasonable, as the cushion will squash down a couple of inches and allow those who are less than lofty to touch the cabin sole with their feet. It is not only uncomfortable to have your feet hanging for any length of time, but in choppy conditions it is nearly impossible to brace yourself. As one of those built for clearing low beams I can vouch for this personally.

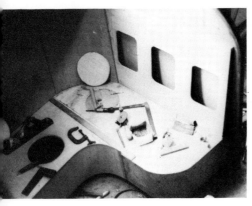

21 & 22:   Saloon area before and after

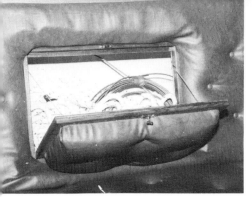
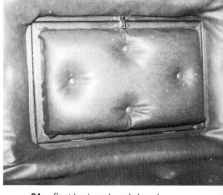

23: Seat-back cupboard open   **24:** Seat-back cupboard closed

The sides of the benches should be higher than the seating surface by an inch or so to contain the cushions. This can also be achieved by adding separate 'fiddles' (*see* Fig. 46).

With the building of almost anything in a boat, strength relies, to some extent, on adequate anchorage. Benches usually run from bulkhead to bulkhead, to which the end framing is screwed and glued, or along the face of a bulkhead as in a dinette, in which case the back framing is fastened the same way (*see* Fig. 47).

In either case the end or back is fastened to the hull where the relevant piece of framing is glassed in (in GRP) or suitably fastened. (*See* chapters on steel and ferro.)

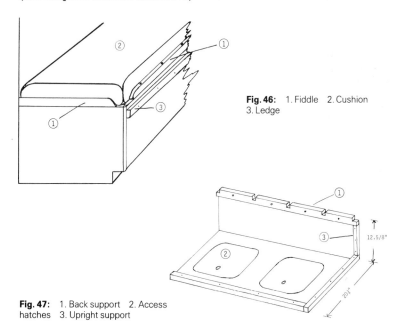

Fig. 46: 1. Fiddle   2. Cushion
3. Ledge

Fig. 47: 1. Back support   2. Access
hatches   3. Upright support

If all other parts are now glued and fastened to each other, the resulting box sections will be firm and stiff and contribute towards the overall strength of the hull.

The most simple saloon (*see* Fig. 45 B) may be all that is possible in narrow hulls; unfortunately they have the disadvantage of needing a table in-between which impedes access forward.

This problem can be alleviated to some extent by having a table with hinged flaps, or by having the table offset towards one bench with one large flap that makes eating possible from the opposite bench when raised, but leaves a passageway when lowered.

On wider hulls a dinette or 'U' shape arrangement can be used, giving the benefit of permanent passage fore and aft, and converting easily into a double berth.

Just as benches on a small boat double as berths, they also create valuable stowage areas, so access should be available through the top and/or the sides or front. Top access is the simplest as it only involves lift-out panels under the cushions, thus avoiding the necessity of making doors.

When making any bench or fixture that is to be covered in, a neat row of 1″ holes around the base will aid air circulation and discourage mould.

Screws that are going to show may be disguised by countersinking, filling or plugging (with wood dowels) or made a feature of by using cup washers. In either case care taken in spacing enhances the visual appeal.

For most built-in furniture, 2″ × 1″ softwood such as deal, preferably selected for being as straight and knot-free as possible, will be adequate for the framing, and exterior grade ply, considerably cheaper than marine grade, for the facing.

Any board material such as ply needs support where weight is going to be put on it. The frequency of the support depends on the thickness of the ply: for ¼″ (6mm) about every foot and for ⅜″ (9mm) about fifteen or sixteen inches. The 2″ × 1″ supports should be used on edge for maximum strength.

Procedure

We will assume that you are now at the stage of having a complete shell with bulkheads and cabin sole, and have chosen your saloon layout.

Whether you are building longitudinal berths running along the hull, or a dinette arrangement with each bench backing on to a bulkhead, the first move will be to fasten the end or back supports (whichever) into the bulkheads at the pre-determined height (*see* Fig. 47). As in the case of floor supports, these will need to be notched to take the longitudinal supports, and this should be done before you glue and screw them into place. These will be cut from the 2″ × 1″ deal framing wood.

For the supports running along the hull there may be a glassed-in stringer that can be utilized. From experience this is seldom the case, however, and should one be the right height at one end of the saloon it rarely is at the other, so it is usually necessary to glass in a fresh support.

It is desirable to have this support upright; as the hull will often be inclined at this point, only the bottom edge will touch. Depending on the angle of the hull, this problem may be overcome by planning a similar angle into the back of the support or filling the gap behind it (*see* Fig. 48). It also has to be notched wherever other supports meet it, and these should be pre-cut before glassing in. Allowance must be made for the thickness of the GRP where you intend to wrap it right over, although it is usually sufficient just to glass in the front, leaving the notches clear (*see* Fig. 48).

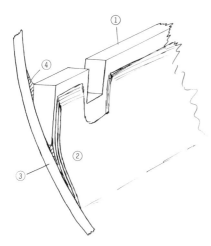

Fig. 48:   1. 2″ × 1″ support   2. Hull
3. CSM   4. Filler

The next step will be to fasten the upright supports to the bulkheads (*see* Fig. 47) and the general outline is now complete.

When three ends of the support frames meet, i.e. a corner formed by two horizontals and an upright, it will often be necessary to cut a section out of a halving joint to allow the third piece to mate up (*see* Fig. 49). On free-standing corners, where this is liable to leave very little wood for fastening, you may prefer to use 2″ × 2″ or two pieces forming an angle (*see* Fig. 50).

If simple box-type benches are being built, the rest of the job merely entails cutting out the top, bottom and corner supports, making sure

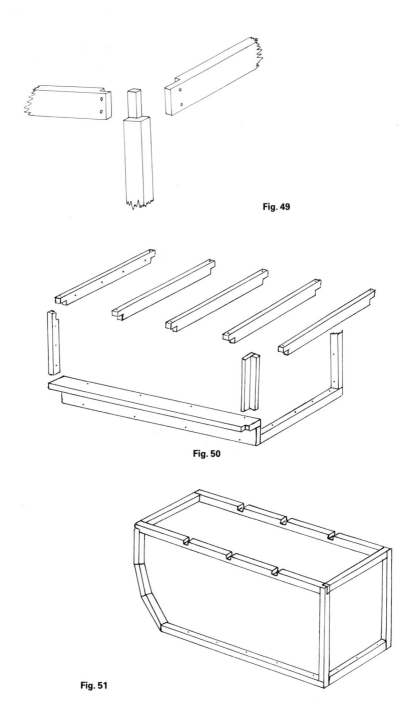

Fig. 49

Fig. 50

Fig. 51

opposing benches are square with each other. The bottom support on dinette benches should be made up to follow the line of the hull from where it meets the cabin sole up to the top support (*see* Fig. 51).

The plywood facing will be glued and pinned to the framework, thus providing vertical support, and if attached with the inside edges just meeting at the corner, a length of quadrant beading can be employed to cover neatly the end grain, making a nice finish (*see* Figs 52 & 52a).

The top 'lift-up' section can be made from one or more pieces with 1″ diameter finger holes conveniently placed. This section can merely rest in position. Bear in mind that each edge of each section must be supported, so if you cut it, do so along the centreline of the frame underneath.

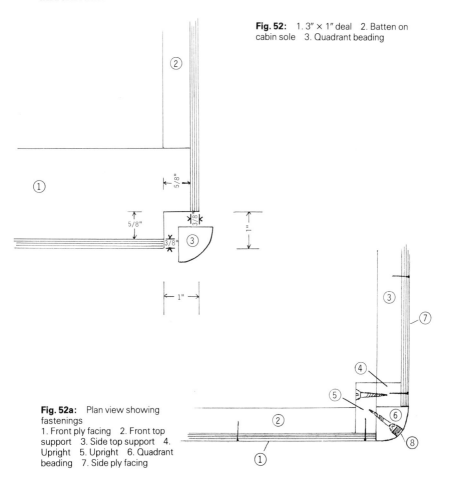

Fig. 52:   1. 3″ × 1″ deal   2. Batten on cabin sole   3. Quadrant beading

Fig. 52a: Plan view showing fastenings
1. Front ply facing   2. Front top support   3. Side top support   4. Upright   5. Upright   6. Quadrant beading   7. Side ply facing

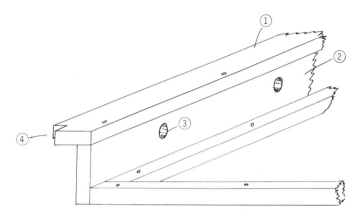

Fig. 53:   1. 3″ × 1″ deal   2. 3″ × 1″ deal   3. Ventilation hole   4. ⅝″ cutaway to take quadrant beading

More elaborate shapes are usually no more than modifications to the simple box, some have a cutaway section at floor level to avoid foot scuffing (*see* Figs. 53 & 54). This type is also quite easy to build using an almost frameless ply construction with internal dividers giving the necessary support. Whichever you choose, making a sketch beforehand indicating the position of all the joints usually shows and clarifies

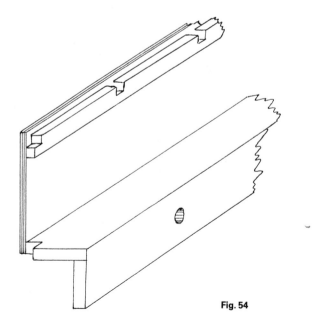

Fig. 54

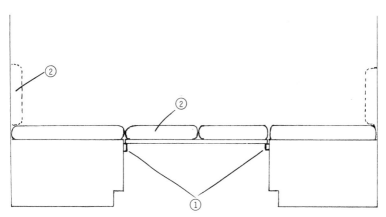

Fig. 55: 1. Ledge 2. Cushions in bed and seat uses

any problems you are likely to encounter. Apart from this, remember that a heavy person imposes quite a strain on a bench, especially in rough conditions, so it usually pays to keep the design simple and strong.

For the box type bench, a kick board of 4″ × ½″ in varnished mahogany around the bottom will take care of shoe marks, and a matching ledge near the top will be necessary to provide support for the edge of the saloon table when this area is going to convert into a double bed (*see* Fig. 55). The height of this ledge is governed by the thickness of the table and the upholstery that will be used to cover it for this function. You should end up with a level and therefore comfortable bed. The upholstered cushions that cover the table area are normally used for backrests to the seats in the daytime.

The galley

Depending on the size of the boat, the galley may be conveniently large, like the bulkhead to bulkhead design illustrated (*see* Fig. 56), or inconveniently small where one or more of the working surfaces doubles as something else outside meal-times, such as one of the steps down into the saloon, or the chart table etc.

If you are going to cook at sea in a single-hulled boat, it will be desirable to have the stove in gimbals, so that it will remain upright regardless of the angle of heel. In motor boats, multihulls or inland cruisers it will need bolting down so that unexpected lurches or bumps can't unseat it. In this latter variety of boats the positioning of the stove fore and aft or athwart is usually a matter of choice, but in sailing boats it is more practical to have it fore and aft for gimballing.

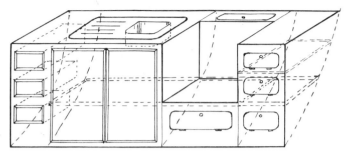

Fig. 56

Attaching the galley to the hull follows the same principle as everything else, as does the framing and/or bulkhead dividers. For instance, the fore and aft galley shown is, in essence, no different to a fore and aft type saloon bench apart from being higher, having access from the front instead of the top, and having a cutaway portion for the stove.

It is based on three dividing bulkheads and its ends are provided by the bulkheads at each end of the main accommodation. The distance between dividers one and two is governed by the width of the stove. This may also include the gimbal pillars. In depth there must be enough room to allow the base of the stove to swing, or in bolted down versions, two or three inches' clearance all round to allow heat from the oven to escape. Bearing the latter in mind, it is safer to line this area with something fireproof such as aluminium or ceramic tiles.

If you haven't yet got the stove but know the dimensions and the height of the gimbal point, the depth can be ascertained by swinging an offcut of hardboard the same size as the side of the stove from this point. Obviously the shallow, two-burner and grill type stove will need much less swinging room than the deeper type with an oven.

To make use of the otherwise redundant space behind the stove is a lift-out panel. Between bulkheads zero and one is a small work top with drawers beneath and between two and three is a stainless steel sink until under which is a large double door cupboard. A dividing shelf runs through to this point. Between three and four are three drawers, the top one being full depth and the bottom quite shallow due to the shape of the hull.

This unit was built into a thirty-one footer; for a smaller boat, however, the unit could be reduced in size by dispensing with area zero to one, or three to four, or both, and the area between two and three could be halved by using a smaller sink unit.

It is usually better to site the stove near to the main companion-way, so that any steam and heat produced by cooking can escape through the door or the sliding hatch above. If this is impracticable a good

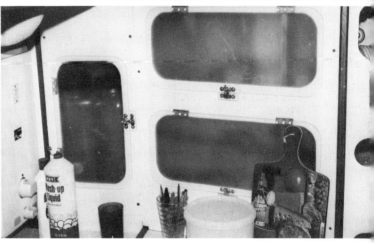

25, 26 & 27: Galley with Perspex doors to cupboard, gimballed stove and ample racks

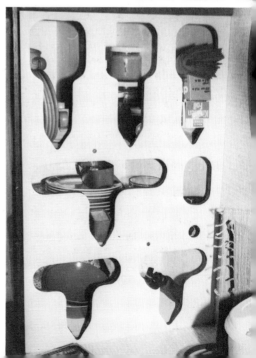

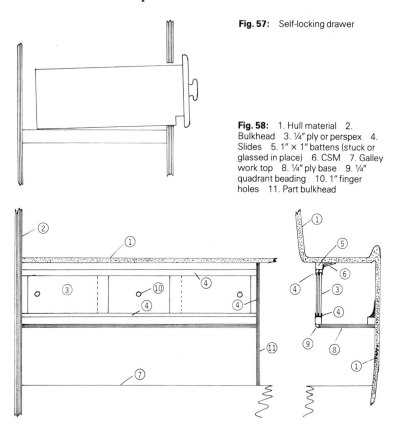

Fig. 57: Self-locking drawer

Fig. 58: 1. Hull material   2. Bulkhead   3. ¼" ply or perspex   4. Slides   5. 1" × 1" battens (stuck or glassed in place)   6. CSM   7. Galley work top   8. ¼" ply base   9. ¼" quadrant beading   10. 1" finger holes   11. Part bulkhead

ventilator, possibly an extractor fan type, should be provided above and also, if possible, an opening portlight or window. Steam or moist air that cannot get clear will create a lot of condensation and promote dampness and mould.

All cupboard doors should be provided with strong catches or sliding bolts when used at sea, and drawers should have turnbuckles or be made self-locking (*see* Fig. 57). The result of ignoring these precautions can be sudden, vicious, chaotic and very demoralizing.

In-between the galley unit and the underside of the side decks there is usually room for more stowage space such as cup and plate racks and shallow cupboards with sliding doors (*see* Fig. 58). If six or eight inches can be left between the top of the galley unit and these cupboards, it will not interfere with the work top area.

For long, low sliding doors such as this, DIY shops sell brown plastic slide channels into which quarter-inch ply fits nice and firmly and doesn't therefore slide too freely.

Roughed up a little with sand-paper the backs of these slides stick very well to the ply or framing wood of the aperture with an epoxy adhesive such as Araldite, and if the fast-setting type is used the pieces can be held by sprung pieces of thin ply (*see* Fig. 59) for thirty minutes or so while curing takes place.

Be sure to get both types of slide—top and bottom—to allow the doors to be fitted or removed easily (*see* Fig. 60).

Some people prefer to use wooden slides for this job, which are available from most timber shops. Whilst I agree that visually they are more pleasing, they often distort or swell if allowed to get damp, causing the doors to stick.

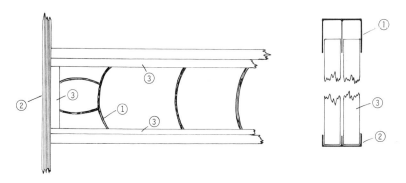

Fig. 59:   1. 3/16″ ply 'springs'
2. Bulkhead   3. Slides

Fig. 60:   1. Top slide   2. Bottom slide   3. Ply or perspex doors

The brown plastic type blend in quite neatly with varnished mahogany or ply, and they are also obtainable in black, white and simulated teak to suit various decors.

The easiest method I have come across for fixing this type of underdeck unit, in cases where it will have no support from underneath, is to make up the dividers, pre-shaped to fit snugly around the obstacles usually found in this area, glassed in stringers etc. Screw and glue the front upright edge support, and have this and the ply suitably notched to take the top and bottom horizontals later, and then fasten the bottom edge support to each divider the same way (*see* Fig. 61).

Now using any convenient method to hold them in the desired position, and making sure that the front and bottom edges of each divider is in line with all the others, fasten them first with filler paste, making a radius and filling any gaps in the usual way, then glass in.

The front horizontals may now be glued and screwed or pinned in place, and the ply bottom cut to shape and fastened. The back edge of the bottom will usually be supported from underneath by a batten that

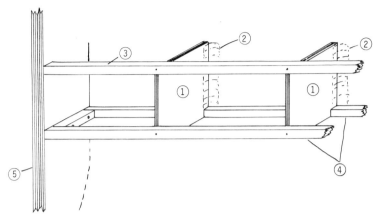

Fig. 61: 1. Ply dividers   2. CSM   3. Top support   4. Bottom supports   5. Bulkhead

will take the top edge of the lining in-between the unit and the work top.

The reason for fixing the bottom first is because the front facing will cover the end grain of the ply, i.e. the quick method, but even better is to mate up the inside edges and fill the corner with quadrant beading. Where the ply is too thin for this to be practical, it is probably better to put the front on first, leave the bottom ply end grain showing and then cover it with ½ round beading pinned into place (*see* Fig. 62).

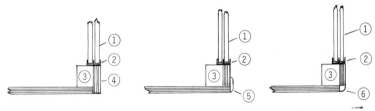

Fig. 62: 1. Sliding doors   2. Door slides   3. Bottom front support   4. Front facing
5. Half-round beading   6. Quadrant beading

When you make the front facing, remember that the top and bottom of the aperture, where sliding doors are concerned, must be parallel. I make a point of mentioning this because the deck will very likely not be parallel to the working surface or whatever underneath.

It will also pay to bear in mind what we discussed about deck support. There is often a long run in-between bulkheads in the saloon/galley area, so instead of making this unit completely hanging it is usually best to include at least one divider around mid-way that

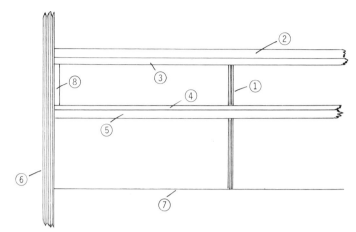

Fig. 63: 1. Part bulkhead division 2. Top front support 3. Top slide 4. Bottom slide 5. Bottom front support 6. Bulkhead 7. Galley work top 8. End slides

meets up with one of the dividing bulkheads of the galley unit (*see* Fig. 63).

You may prefer to have an L-shaped galley, and although just as easy to make, using the same methods, there is always the problem of the corner. This often becomes wasted space at the worst, and inaccessible at the best unless you can have access from the top. Domestic kitchens suffer the same problem, and often utilize a plastic covered wire unit that is attached to the door containing the contents. This does, however, rob you of quite a bit of usable space.

One thing that does use this space to advantage is a small, top opening chest type fridge, such as the one marketed by Camping Gaz. Be careful though, to have the specified gap all round for ventilation, and access for lighting etc.

Forward berth units

This is a tricky little number as the boat usually curves in all directions at this point, making it difficult to find levels.

As for construction of other built-in units, the first step is to find a datum point. This is a point that you know is true and from which verticals or horizontals may be found. This will almost certainly be the forward main bulkhead in this case, as it will be vertical and at right angles to the keel centreline.

The simplest method for finding the datum point is to fasten a batten at the desired height from one side to the other, ignoring for the

28: Forward double berth allowing standing space (left), hatches and a bulkhead watertight hatch through to chain locker

Fig. 64: 1. Hull 2. Beam shelf 3. Support beams 4. F'ward berth cabin sole 5. Toilet and shower cabin sole level

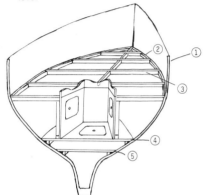

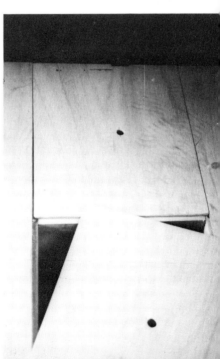

29 & 30: Framing for a double berth allowing use of large removable hatches

moment that it goes right across the entrance. Don't glue it at this point, just screw it lightly into place on one side, and then, resting a spirit-level on it, clamp it to the entrance with a G-cramp, taking care to use a small offcut to avoid making a dent in the bulkhead. Now screw the other side home.

With the use of a spirit-level and a long batten, a series of marks may be made with a felt-tip pen or pencil (the former marks GRP well) down both sides of the compartment, all of which will be level with the datum batten.

Before going any further, check the clearance between the underside of the forward deck and a point about six inches above your marks. You need at least two and preferably three feet to bend your knees in bed or to crawl to the chain locker.

The position of the support frames depends a lot on the shape of the boat, but the usual layout is for two bunks starting either side of a small standing area, (*see* Fig. 64) and joining up from there forward.

The framing is applied in the same way as the foredeck beams, with a notched shelf each side, fore and aft, cross beams slotting into it, and either a central beam as illustrated (*see* Fig. 64), or two that start at the main bulkhead and meet lower down.

There is a large amount of stowage space available under the forward berths and you may wish to divide it athwart with one or more bulkheads. If so, these should be fitted before the fore and aft beams, and glassed in as for all bulkheads taking care to avoid high spots in the hull.

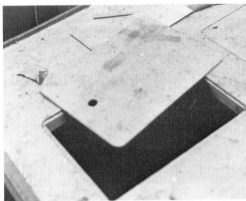

32: A hatch lid and the framing on which it sits

31: A useful size of bedroom locker; this is covered in Draylon (as is the bulkhead) which gives a 'cosy' effect. Battening is added last

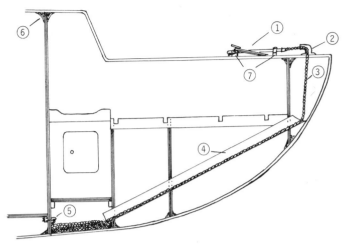

Fig. 65:   1. Anchor   2. Chain pipe   3. Chain   4. 4″ PVC pipe   5. 'U' bolt   6. CSM
7. Anchor chocks

Before much more is done here, holes should be cut in the dividing
bulkhead/s to take the anchor chain pipe, (4″ PVC drain pipe with or
without a slow bend depending on the run is good for this job, *see* Fig.
65). If you have a lot of chain which amounts to a considerable weight,
it is a good idea to lead it back aft and low down where it will not affect
stability or forward buoyancy and will not encourage pitching. On the
other hand, if you have only two or three fathoms joined onto rope, the
forward chain locker will probably cope.

As through-bolting would be unsightly, the side beam shelf is
usually just glassed in, and therefore serves a function as an additional
stringer. Where there are plenty of stringers already, it is not always

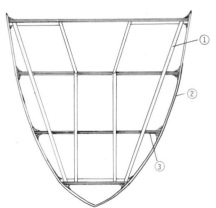

Fig. 66:   1. Berth supports   2. Hull
3. Dividing bulkheads (notched to take
supports)

necessary for these shelves to be glassed in at all, in which case they can be mounted in a straight line (*see* Fig. 66) provided they are strong enough to take the weight, i.e. maybe 3″ or 4″ × 1½″ where there is no dividing bulkhead to give support.

The top panels should be lift-up to give access, and this saves the necessity of putting doors in the facing panels (*see* Figs. 64 & 65). The latter should be built up three or four inches above the beams to contain the mattresses.

Linings

If you made your own deck and superstructure, the internal surfaces will look a lot better than GRP, and it may suit you merely to paint them. However, insulation may be necessary if you are spending much time on board and being harassed by condensation.

There are many different materials available with which to do this job, some cheaper than others. There are different methods too, giving a great scope for personal choice, budget and time availability.

The quickest and most basic covering is a thick, anti-condensation paint, containing cork or mica chippings which is merely painted straight on. The overall effect is practical rather than aesthetic, as the inside surface of GRP is usually fairly uneven due to overlaps and these still show through.

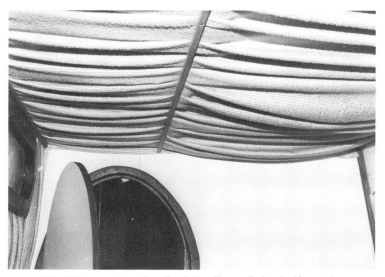

33: Toilet compartment head liner in towelling, easily detached for washing

Some areas can be covered quite effectively by ceramic tiles, foam-backed or ordinary vinyl, or even linoleum stuck directly to the GRP (which is scored and cleaned first). It really depends on the area involved. For instance, anti-condensation paint is perfectly adequate for the insides of cupboards or toilet compartments and areas where the visual aspect is not so important.

For overhead areas, sticking any sheet material up with contact adhesive constitutes my idea of a nightmare. Fighting gravity in this way takes guts and determination and seldom looks really good.

If you wish to use vinyl, or any board material (ply etc.) it is much easier to screw pre-shaped panels up into battens glassed to the deckhead. The battens can be placed at regular intervals and held in place by props while curing, taking care to cover anything underneath that might be dripped on.

Vinyl may be stuck with contact adhesive to the ply, and wrapped round the edges (*see* Fig. 67) and then screwed up into place. When all the panels are up, the line of screws are easily covered by varnished mahogany battens or similar, and the screws holding these up may be either counter-sunk and filled (or plugged with dowels) or left on the surface in cup washers. The latter method is often more practical because the panels can easily be removed, which may become necessary if you wish to run a length of wire to a new light, or fix a deck vent etc.

My own preference is for tongued, grooved and V'd pine (TGV) which gives a nice, warm feel to the interior. When this method of lining is used, the fixing battens will have to run across the deckhead,

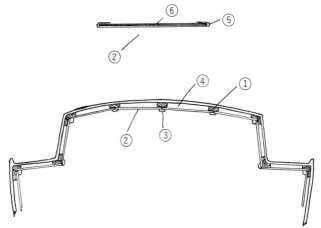

Fig. 67:   1. Battens stuck or glassed   2. Lining panels   3. Decorative trim battens or beading to cover joins   4. Air or insulation space   5. Vinyl (plain or foam-backed)   6. Thin (3/16″) ply

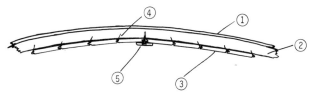

Fig. 68: 1. Hull   2. Deck beam or batten   3. TGV planks   4. Hidden fastening pins
5. Central trim batten

with a fore and aft one down each corner. One cross batten every two
feet should suffice.

If the deckhead is rectangular, as in some canal craft, it is feasible to
start from each side and work up to the centre plank, which can be
sprung into place (if you have been lucky or clever enough to end up
with a full plank); otherwise, any resultant gap can be covered by a
mahogany or pine (your choice) beam.

However, most deckheads are anything but rectangular, and because of this I have found it easier to work from the centreline down to
each side (*see* Fig. 68) where the outer plank or two are cut in a long
taper to suit the edge of the deckhead. The side lining will then come
up and cover any slight discrepancies.

Any apertures through the lining, such as windows, ventilators or
hatches, must be framed with battens or timber the same thickness.
The rules are the same, no edges must be left without support
underneath.

The gap in-between the deckhead or inner surfaces and the lining
may be left as an air gap, or filled with insulation. There are different
schools of thought on this subject. Some people reckon an air gap

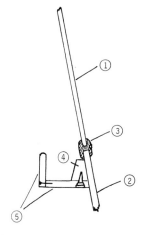

Fig. 69: 1. Window   2. Coaming   3.
Rubber mounting channel   4. Wood
batten stuck or glassed   5. Wood
forming drip tray

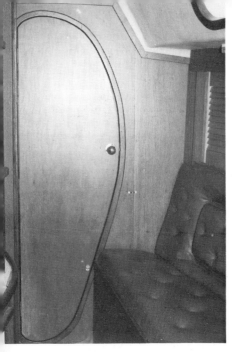

34: Doors don't have to be symmetric – shoulders are wider than feet

could fill up with moist air and promote rot, although if the wood is pre-treated it should be safe enough. Others fill the gap with panels of expanded polystyrene, but the fire risk this involves doesn't appeal to me; polyurethane foam, although more expensive, would be safer here. Loft type insulation such as Cosywrap solves the fire hazard problem but could be vulnerable to dampness in the event of a leak from above. One method which seems to overcome most of these snags is to use Cosywrap sealed into polythene sausages.

When using varnished, decorative or ply panels covered in material of some sort, $^{3}/_{16}''$ thickness will normally be sufficient, and will bend into shape without problem.

Whichever method you decide to use, there is no doubt that good insulation helps to combat condensation and makes life aboard a lot more bearable in the winter. Condensation occurs when warm, moist air comes into contact with a cold surface; windows can therefore be a problem, but not much can be done about this without some form of temporary double-glazing, and this often hampers ventilation which is vital in a small area. Built-in drip trays which drain overboard or which may be sponged out daily is often the best answer (*see* Fig. 69).

When using varnished, decorative or ply panels covered in material of some sort, $^{3}/_{16}''$ thickness will normally be sufficient, and will bend into shape without problem.

Foam padding can be used under material to give a nice spongy feel to panels, and a button-down effect can be created here quite easily. It is normal to 'back' the foam with $^{3}/_{16}''$ ply, and by drilling two holes in the back close together, nylon line can be threaded through the eye of the button and the single hole in the front, drawn through each hole at the back and tied off.

Doors

The most basic door is simply cut out from a ply facing, the cut-out becoming the door. With a power jigsaw it is possible to ease the blade through the ply by starting with it almost parallel. In practice I have found this method only occasionally successful, as the blade is flexible and often distorts. On the other hand, if you drill a hole large enough to take the blade and start your cut, it will show up badly in the finished job. Consequently I have found the best way is to drill a line of very small holes, for about ⅜", and run these in together by carefully re-drilling at different angles until a slot is formed just long enough to take the jigsaw blade. If this slot is made to come under the eventual position of a hinge or catch, it will be effectively hidden.

The corners of the door will have to be radiused so that the saw can do the job in one continuous cut, and great care is needed to steer the saw around these corners without going wide of the line. Jigsaws are difficult enough to steer in any case, but control is easier if you cut slowly and use a sharp blade. When the blade blunts (and the resin in ply does this quite quickly) and you start pushing the saw, control becomes impossible. Any pressure should be downwards, to stop the saw from vibrating up and down and thereby reducing its effectiveness.

As with any cut in ply, it is better to cut from the back so as not to splinter the face side.

All doors need door stops against which to close, and these will normally be fastened behind the facing (*see* Fig. 70 A). One alternative

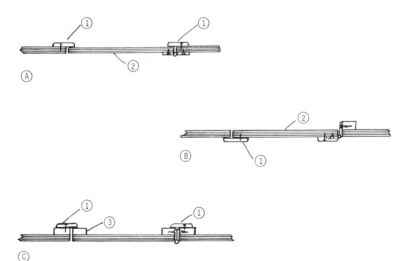

Fig. 70: 1. Door stop battens   2. Door   3. Frame

is to make up a flange from ply or mahogany offcuts which is glued and pinned to the front face of the door and is about an inch larger all round (*see* Fig. 70 B).

A door of this type may, of course, have a frame on the back for reinforcement, and if there is also a frame behind the facing, the hinges can be used conventionally (*see* Fig. 70 C), but hinges should not be screwed into the end grain of ply as this will create a weak fastening, so where the door is frameless the hinges are best attached across the face (*see* Fig. 70 A). Where you use the flange method they can be hidden (*see* Fig. 70 B).

Hinges should be brass or nylon, or some other equally non-corrodible material. Many cheaper types do not have stainless steel or brass pins, so it is better to pay the extra and buy marine quality. The best ones are often obtainable second-hand where an elderly boat is being broken up.

On account of the price of decent hinges, they can be dispensed with in a lot of cases, as in Fig. 71. Here, the door stop battens are attached to the inside of the facing at the sides, and the top (optional). A batten is attached to the inside of the door along the bottom edge, it should protrude an inch or so. As this batten hooks over the bottom of the facing, it should be cut short enough to clear the door stops. The door is held in place by a simple turnbuckle fastened to the top of the facing. This method is only suitable for cupboard and similar sized doors.

Louver-doors are attractive, good for ventilation, and can be purchased ready-made in pine or hardwood. A lot of these, suitably

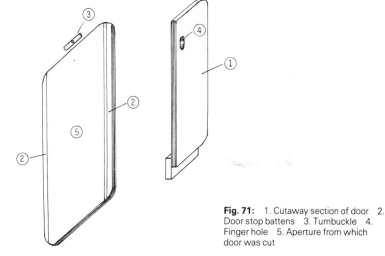

Fig. 71: 1. Cutaway section of door   2. Door stop battens   3. Turnbuckle   4. Finger hole   5. Aperture from which door was cut

35: Readily available louvered doors in slides

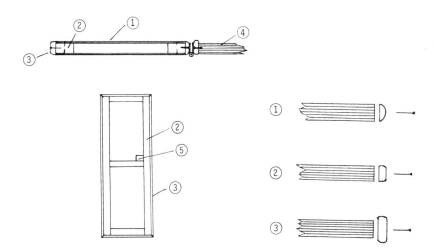

Fig. 72: 1. 3/16″ ply (glued and pinned to frame) 2. Frame timber 3. Edging to cover frame and ply 4. Bulkhead 5. Lock block to give extra depth if using key type lock

Fig. 72a: 1. Half round 2. Rectangular section (rounded corners) 3. Oversize (all corners rounded)

36: A thin strip of 3/16″ ply used for the surround. Cut across the grain to facilitate bending. Edges sanded round and painted

37: Cupboard doors and apertures look neat when the end grain of the ply is covered with teak or mahogany trim. The trim can be flush or stand proud. In this case, the corners are rounded and made from separate pieces routered out of solid. A small fretsaw or coping-saw can be used in the absence of a router. (**See also** photos 61 and 62.)

protected with gloss or matt varnish or paint, are quite suitable for internal use, but if you intend to buy this type of door for the main companion-way or entrance, make sure it is well jointed at the corners, and not just held by dowelling pegs, and be sure to apply a complete varnish or paint system before exposing to the elements. These doors can be hinged normally, or the short ones used in sliding tracks (make sure the slides are deeper at the top for fitting and removal).

Full-length doors will often tend to distort unless they are ¾″ thick or so, and sometimes even ply of this size will bend after a while. Obviously to fit a timber frame here will begin to make the whole thing a bit thick and clumsy, so the alternative is to make a double-skinned

38: Unbreakable glass in main companion-way admits more light

39: Useful bedside cupboards and shelves

door from two thin sheets, perhaps ³⁄₁₆″ ply (*see* Fig. 72). Doors like this can be left hollow, or the spaces filled with panels of polyurethane foam, in which case they become quite soundproof, provided they are a good fit. Needless to say, the ply panels are glued and pinned to the frame.

Some people like the end grain of ply as a feature, when smoothed and varnished. Others don't. For those who don't there are two alternatives: either make doors as already described and paint them so the end grain is not apparent, or fit timber edging (*see* Fig. 72a).

This is very easy in the case of square cornered doors, merely a case of gluing and pinning a ³⁄₈″ or maybe ½″ hardwood strip, the same width as the thickness of the ply, having previously cut it to shape with a mitre in each corner. The door frame is treated in the same way, and the finished effect is quite classy. The door, when this is done, must be the size of the aperture minus twice the thickness of the edging, minus about another $\frac{1}{16}''$ for clearance. Punch the pins below the surface with a small-headed nail punch. The holes, filled with a matching colour filler, will then virtually vanish, and plane blades won't be damaged if the edge needs trimming down a little.

Timber edging can be fitted to oval doors, but only where the radius is large, unless you want to enter the realms of steam bending, and the edging must be very thin and pliable, maybe only $\frac{1}{8}''$ or so. Steaming is not that difficult, by the way, all that is needed is a length of drain-pipe (cast-iron) into which steam from a kettle can be fed. The steam can be conveyed through armoured plastic pipe with rags used as stuffing at both the end where the plastic pipe enters and the other end. After a while the wood becomes very supple, but the length of time depends very much on the steam supply and the thickness of the timber. A little experimentation will be necessary. While the wood is supple, bend it around the door and either pin it into place straight

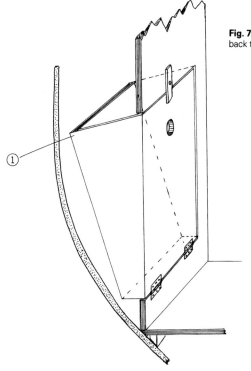

Fig. 73:   1. Hopper, slopes down at back to facilitate opening

away, or wait until it is dry, remove it, apply glue and replace and fasten it.

There are places on board where, owing to the shape of the hull, a cupboard is virtually useless because there is little or no depth at the bottom. This is a case for the hopper type door (*see* Fig. 73) which may be hinged or hooked at the bottom and held by a turnbuckle at the top.

By this method the hopper can be of maximum size. If the door was hinged at the side the hopper would have to be cut back in width at the swinging side to prevent it from fouling the frame.

Door handles

These vary from simple finger holes to quite elaborate and decorative fastenings, as any marine catalogue will show.

This is obviously very much a matter of personal choice, and budget. Maybe the only point to bear in mind is that they should never be sharp or project too far where they might impale an overbalancing sailor.

Handles are simple to make from offcuts of timber (*see* Fig. 74), and are also strong and cheap.

Door locks and catches

DIY shop catches are readily available, but as for hinges, make sure the parts are non-corrodible i.e. brass, plastic or stainless steel.

The size of the catch depends on the size of the door, and the weight of gear behind it that might try to break out during a sudden lurch. Locks are secure, but expensive in brass. Sliding bolts are a lot cheaper and also strong. Brass turnbuckles built into a split circle are also good (the segment with the turnbuckle is attached to the frame, not the door), but need a certain amount of friction to keep them in place, as do turnbuckles on their own, and for this reason they always leave marks on the door.

On full length doors, brass or nylon ball catches work quite well, especially the adjustable type, if you don't feel like going to the expense of a brass mortise-lock. Sliding bolts are no use here if the

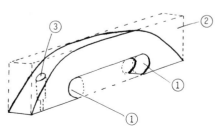

Fig. 74: 1. 1″ diameter hole 2. 8″ offcut 3. Countersunk fastening hole

door needs to be opened from either side. If domestic fittings are used for economy, be prepared to dismantle and oil them regularly, particularly if the boat is exposed to the salty sea air.

Saloon tables

These can be roughly divided into two categories, those that convert the saloon area into a double bed, and those that don't.

The former must obviously be made exactly the right size to sit on the ledges fitted to the saloon benches, and be strong enough to span two or three feet and take the weight of a couple of bodies. The back edge can admittedly rest on a ledge if one has been built for the purpose, but any support for the front would need to be strictly temporary, or it would hamper access to the seats when in normal use.

The simple design of table illustrated (*see* Fig. 75) is of ¾″ exterior quality ply (18mm) with mahogany edging doubling as fiddles (2″ × ½″ prepared) and two corners cut from a small offcut of mahogany planking of ¾″ thickness the same radius as the ply and same depth as the fiddles. By this method, the fiddles can be straight for simplicity, and there are two gaps for clearing the table of crumbs. The top is just under three feet in width, and four feet long.

Underneath is one folding leg, which fits into a raised slot in the floor so that it can't be kicked under and collapse the table. Two four-inch brass hinges secure the 'T' piece at the top of the leg to a 3″ × 1″ mahogany batten screwed and glued to the underside of the table.

The table is secured, at the shelving end, by two galvanized fittings—usually found on garden gates—with the rounded heads cut off which fit into two corresponding holes drilled into mahogany pads

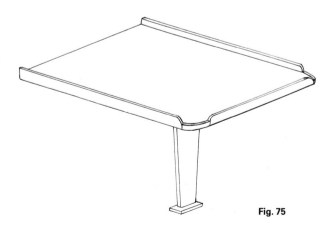

Fig. 75

fastened to each corner. (These fittings are only about ten pence each.) A sliding bolt at each side keeps the table locked down as a precaution against any crew member trying to make a quick getaway.

There are now numerous sliding pillar and pump-up hydraulic table supports on the market, which are very strong, and priced accordingly, but a simple version of the same thing can be made out of timber, and is of ample strength provided the timber is of sufficient size (*see* Fig. 76).

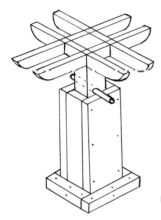

Fig. 76

The table top, in this instance, is designed to slot into a U-shape saloon bench arrangement. The single leg is of 4″ × 4″ hardwood, and slides up and down a trunking of the same material. An eight-inch length of iron rod through one of three holes in the leg rests on top of the trunking to pin the table at the required height, and when the pin is withdrawn the top slides down to the same height as the benches, and so forms a double bed area.

On the underside of the table there is a timber fabrication (*see* Fig. 76) to which the top of the leg is fastened.

Depending on the height required, the leg may need to slide down below floor level when the table is depressed, so make sure sufficient space exists underneath.

The gangway type table is not normally used for bed conversion. This is usually in-between who longitudinal benches which are merely used as separate bunks when needed.

Designs are numerous, but there is generally a drop-leaf arrangement on one side or both to allow access forward. Legs need to be fairly strong and fastened securely to the floor (in sea-going boats). The top can either be made up of ply edged with mahogany, or solid mahogany planks. The latter are often available in ten-inch widths,

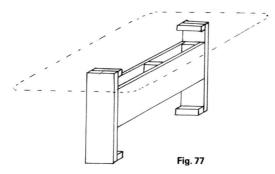

Fig. 77

and so a top and two leaves would provide an overall width of two foot six inches. If anything wider is required ply is probably the best bet. I mention mahogany, by the way, because it is one of the cheapest hardwoods available, and easy to work. It also varnishes up a similar colour to sapele-faced ply. Of course, if your purse runs to it, there are many other suitable woods, e.g. teak, or its similar but cheaper cousins iroko, afrormosia, utile etc. Timber importers are often able to make offers on certain types.

In small boats, stowage built into the table is often useful (*see* Fig. 77) and also provides support halfway down. Alternative stowage can also be built into the top, and the centre section hinged for access (*see* Fig. 78).

Chart tables

Often the saloon table or even the kitchen work top has to double as a chart table, but where there is space for a permanent or fold-away arrangement, it does come in useful, especially for sea work, and it isn't robbed of its function at meal-times.

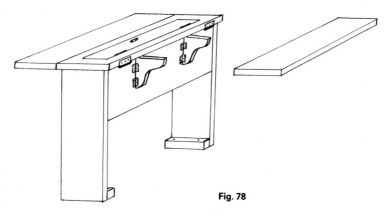

Fig. 78

40 & 41: A useful size of chart table, raised and lowered

42: Chart table with secure seating for navigator

44: Handholds help on long steps

43: Main companion-way steps bracketed and bolted for security

Ideally, the table should be large enough on which to open up a full size Admiralty chart, but this is normally too big to fit anywhere on smallish boats, so a 'half chart' size has to suffice. It is handy if there is space underneath to stow a number of charts, as this will keep them well protected. Access to the charts can be by means of a hinged or lift-out top, or a drawer.

Steps down to saloon

This will normally concern the main entrance from the cockpit down into the saloon.

The size, shape and number of steps varies enormously in different boats. A deep keel sailing boat, for instance, with a shallow, self-draining cockpit and a bridge deck may well have a saloon cabin sole five or six feet down from the bridge deck, and need a fairly conventional set of steps. On the other hand, a small motor cruiser with a centrally mounted engine may only need one or two steps down, and these will often be part of the engine box (*see* Fig. 79).

Whatever kind of steps you need, they will be in constant use, and must therefore be very strong. Apart from the possibility of bearing heavy people, those in a sea-going boat will often be used to support a member of the crew in rough conditions, who may be halfway up or down when the boat lurches violently. This is not so much of a problem when the steps are fixed, but they seldom are, because

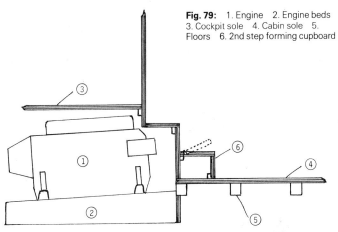

Fig. 79: 1. Engine   2. Engine beds 3. Cockpit sole   4. Cabin sole   5. Floors   6. 2nd step forming cupboard

usually all or part of them will need removing for engine access. Temporary fixtures, therefore, must be good. This is no place for economy. At points like the top of the steps where you might be tempted to secure them with a hook and eye, or sliding bolt on one side, lash out and buy another for the other side. Also, make sure that the base of the steps is well secured by fitting into flush or raised slots in the cabin sole.

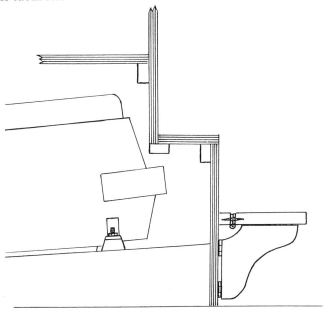

Fig. 80

In small boats of any kind, the steps often intrude inconveniently into the accommodation, especially where the galley is just inside. This could mean that the duty cook has to stand at an awkward angle to operate, and may become uncomfortable or unenthusiastic or both. This can frequently be avoided by a hinged bottom step (*see* Fig. 80) that folds away flat when not in use. The supports can be made from offcuts of ply, or 1″ pine planking, and three are better than two. The spacing of the hinges on the step an inch or so away from the engine box is to allow the supports to be cleared by it when swung down.

Steps can also provide good stowage, with one or more forming a cupboard with a lift-up lid (*see* Fig. 79).

As you can see, a certain amount of ingenuity and cunning is called for here; steps can be much more than things on which to tread, but only if you give them sound anchorage points, beefy hinges (where used) and good support under steps or lids.

Engine boxes

As we have seen, these may be part of the companion-way steps, or they may be a separate construction out in the cockpit. Of course, in many designs, especially larger, deep centre boats, they will not be necessary at all, as there will be a complete engine compartment, with access via a lift-up hatch or from some part of the interior.

Those boats that need a box often have them out in the open, therefore they must be weather-proof. At the same time, though, they must allow sufficient ventilation for the engine to breathe. Diesels especially will run rough or give up altogether if starved of air. Mechanics will tell you it is not uncommon to be called out to diagnose the fault on a badly running engine only to find that it runs perfectly as soon as the engine box lid is lifted. The box should also be easy to dismantle for access to all parts of the engine, and again, strong enough to be sat upon, as it undoubtedly will be if it is the right height (*see* Fig. 81).

Finally, some sort of soundproofing is desirable, long hours of listening to a noisy engine can be tiring as well as irritating. This normally means lining the box with insulation material. There are proprietary brands on the market which are amazing in their absorption qualities, but as with anything good, they are not cheap. A DIY alternative is to make the box on a double skin principle, i.e. two layers of ¼″ ply separated by 1″ framing, and stuff the gap with glass wool, normally sold for loft insulation. There are also sound absorption panels sold by car accessory shops which are quite effective. Don't use anything inflammable, and for petrol engines particularly, line the inside of the box with asbestos or alloy sheeting.

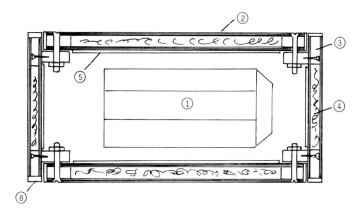

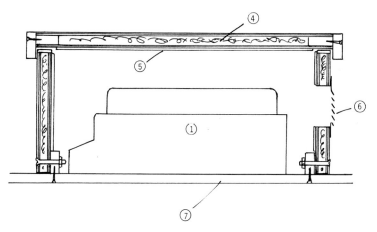

Fig. 81: 1. Engine   2. ¼″ ply   3. Pine frame   4. Insulation   5. Asbestos or alloy
6. Louvered vent   7. Cockpit sole   8. Edging to cover end grain

Alloy or brass louvered vents will cope with the air supply and keep out the rain.

Instrument consoles

There are two definite fields of thought on instrumentation. Some people put banks of dials on a console that wouldn't look out of place on Concorde, while others have, perhaps, an oil pressure gauge often mounted out of sight on the engine.

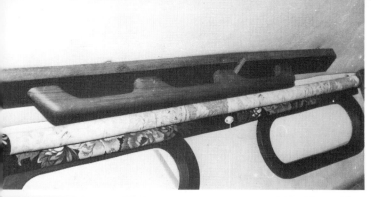

45: Internal handhold bolted through to external one. Note also the use of roller blinds for pairs of windows

46: Upright tubular pillars make good handholds as well as bracing up half bulkheads and coachroofs

Somewhere in-between these two extremes is a happy medium where five or six dials fit happily into a console near the wheel.

In boats where there is no shelter near the steering position, the console is often mounted on the main bulkhead or some handy and visually accessible place, behind a waterproof panel.

Apart from protection from the elements, which is essential to most modern materials and instruments whether they profess to be weather-proof or not, it is important to have easy access to the back of the panel for maintenance and repair. The bulkhead panel, therefore, must have an entrance from the back, and the console by the wheel should lift or hinge. (*See* page 167, photos 61 & 62.)

A typical console hinges at the top, and each panel below the wheel position is removable, giving plenty of room to get at the fuses, the steering gear, Morse Teleflex cables etc.

Grab rails and handles

Even on flat water boats move a little, in the wash of a passing boat, for instance. For this reason it is a sound safety measure to have something to grab hold of to keep your balance.

Their very function means that handles should be strong and easy to hold, i.e. large enough for the biggest fingers, and strategically placed.

It is often possible to build handles into steps and furniture. At the risk of being basic, they are very necessary in roomy toilet compartments at sea, for use in both sitting and standing positions.

Very likely there will be provision for grab rails along either side of the superstructure, and it is a good idea, where possible, to duplicate these on the inside, in which case matching rails can be through-bolted (*see* Photo 45). In any case, handles should be bolted or at least glued and screwed securely.

Wooden rails are quite easy to make (*see* Fig. 82), from hardwood preferably, or strong softwood such as Douglas fir. To save on timber, two rails can be cut out of the same piece if it is half as wide again as the height of the rail; one 4″ × 1½″ prepared plank, for example, will make two decent sized rails. Handles of similar shape can usually be made from offcuts (*see* Fig. 74).

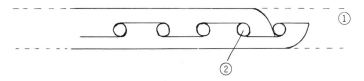

Fig. 82:   1. 4″ × 1½″ timber   2. 1½″ diameter holes

Another useful addition to the interior for handholds are pillars. These usually consist of an alloy or chrome tube, 1″ in diameter, with a flange at each end, and usually fastened somewhere convenient from work top height to the deckhead. This also serves to give the coachroof extra support.

A stouter version of the same idea is often used as an internal mast support in small, open-plan boats, from under the mast support pad down to the cabin sole, directly over a floor in contact with the keel, or reinforced for the purpose.

6 · Tools and carpentry

Tools necessary

Power
Jigsaw
Drill, preferably ½″, at least ⅜″ chuck
Circular saw
(The above may be attachments to the drill if really necessary.)
Router (handy but not essential)
Orbital sander (handy but not essential)
Drill bits: assortment for steel and wood
Blades for jigsaw: assortment for steel and wood

Hand
Tenon-saw
Rip-saw (where power saw unavailable)
Coping-saw (where jigsaw unavailable)
Fretsaw (where jigsaw unavailable)
Hack-saw
Hand drill (useful for cabinet work)
Brace (where power drill unavailable)
Smoothing plane
Jack-plane
Screwdrivers: electrical
                small, medium and large
                Philips
                pump (useful but pricey)
Chisels: selection 1½″ down to ¼″
Bevel
Set square
Mitre block
Steel tape-measure

Spirit-levels: Small and large
Rasp or dreadnought files: flat, ½ round and round
G-cramps
Sash-cramps
Hammers: claw, small, etc. Also nail punch.
Mallet
Adjustable spanner
Oilstone
Workmate bench or static bench and vice

Needless to say, the list could be endless. I would like to be able to say that you won't need half of these tools, but I can't. In fact, you will probably find the need for more, however, I don't suppose many people just go out and buy a complete set of tools. It is far more normal to make a start with the basic essentials and buy or borrow as the need arises.

Sash-cramps and G-cramps are a good example of items that won't always be necessary in large quantities, and they are both expensive, so borrowing or hiring could be the answer.

I have found that most people are wary about lending tools, mostly with good reason. An amazing amount of people borrow with every intention of speedy return, but after a few days or weeks have elapsed their attitude seems to change to one of ownership. Indeed, one is often met with abuse on asking for its return. There are a few trusting souls around, I used to be one myself until experience made me take a more cynical approach to all but trusted friends.

Bearing all this in mind, it pays dividends to offer a cash deposit around the value of the tool in question. If you are genuine you will get it back, and if not, the owner can replace it without personal loss.

Lending power tools can be expensive in repairs and lost time, and many other tools can be spoiled or blunted through misuse. In these cases it is fair to offer replacement, this way, the owner may lend you tools again.

Carpentry—general advice

This is not essentially a book on carpentry, and I am not officially qualified to give lessons. I have, however, come up against and had to overcome numerous snags in the course of building the interiors of a few boats, a few domestic kitchens, company reception areas, built-in wardrobe units etc., all of which are similar in technique if they differ in required strength and materials.

The most general advice I can give is not to hurry, and to use very sharp tools. I worked in a boatyard once for two or three years, and learned a great deal from my boss, who I took to be a lifetime, traditional shipwright. This seemed a fairly logical assumption because he had a very good name locally, and spent a lot of time repairing wooden boats, from dinghy to trawler size. It turned out that he had been a disillusioned salesman not that many years before who had made one or two items of furniture by way of a hobby.

The first thing he taught me was how to sharpen tools, and amazingly, all the jobs with which I had had such difficulty for so long suddenly became easier. The need to press hard with plane, chisel, hand saw or power saw makes it almost impossible to be accurate.

Probably the next most important thing is measuring. The old maxim that it is better to measure twenty times and cut once, rather than vice versa, is very true. Careful measurement and lack of haste combined with (extremely) sharp tools will make a good carpenter out of someone who thought they were very mediocre.

Practice makes perfect, so it makes sense to start off with the basics and leave the prettying up until later.

Hand saws
Use as much of the blade as possible in a nice even stroke. It only cuts on the pushing stroke so draw it back lightly. Try to work up a slow rhythm, at a pace that doesn't tire you out. Don't hold the handle too tightly or you will almost certainly go off line.

When cutting to length, err on the long side, i.e. cut down the outside of your pencil line. You can always take off more wood, however awkward it might be, but you can't replace it.

When cutting a halving joint where there is a knot, or where the grain dives downwards, make a lot of cuts (*see* Fig. 83). This makes it much easier to chisel out the surplus without taking out too much wood.

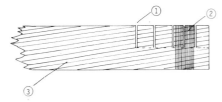

Fig. 83:   1. Saw cuts   2. Knot
3. Direction of grain

Power saws
Circular saw: power tools take a considerable amount of the hard work out of carpentry, but they take a bit of getting used to. Steering is not that easy, especially when the blade has lost its edge a little, and the resin in plywood brings this about very quickly.

Circular saws are not always that accurate, and the width of the cut has to be taken into consideration. For cutting board material (i.e.

ply) it is usually better to cut oversize and plane the edge flat and true afterwards.

This kind of saw has one very good quality in that it will cut at a constant depth. This makes halving joints a lot easier, especially when there are several to do, and also cutting slots for shelves and steps (*see* Fig. 84).

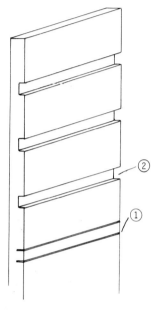

Fig. 84: 1. Saw cuts 2. After chiselling out

Jigsaw: an extremely useful tool for numerous cutting jobs, but technique is needed. It is always very tempting to push, but almost impossible to keep straight if you do. If anything, pressure should be downwards to keep the bottom plate firmly on the wood. If it is allowed to vibrate up and down efficiency will be lost.

Most of the cheap ones rev too fast, which makes the blade go up and down too quickly to unclog itself. Constant switching off slows it down, but probably does no good at all to the mechanism. A two-speed version is not much more expensive, and the slow speed is more efficient.

Jigsaws cut on the up stroke, so when cutting ply they often tear out splinters as they cut. This can be prevented to some extent by using a fine cutting blade (and a sharp one!), but better still, cut from what will be the inside where possible.

When cutting thinnish ply, only a small amount of the blade will be used. You will see how much, because that portion will go shiny, and the bottom part will still be untouched. If you have access to a bench grinder, snap an inch or so off the part that fits into the saw, grind the teeth down so it fits into the slot, and you now have a new blade, even if it is a little shorter—but this doesn't matter for cutting the sort of thicknesses of which these machines are capable. Make sure, though, that the required length of blade still protrudes below the baseplate at its shortest position.

Power drill
This is probably the most universal tool, particularly because it has the capability of running circular saw or jigsaw attachments. It must be borne in mind, though, that attachments are really a compromise, and you can't expect them to be as good as the real thing. Nevertheless, if you are operating on a really tight budget, they can still save a lot of muscle work.

The power of a drill, or any other machine, depends on the size of its motor. Usually you get what you pay for, so if you buy the cheapest and give it a lot of hard work, don't be too surprised if it burns out fairly quickly. Bigger motors will cope with tougher assignments and stand up to more abuse.

Bearing this in mind, and this goes for all power tools, but especially the weaker ones, use them with consideration. When drilling, use sharp drills, and in the case of deep holes, withdraw the drill every

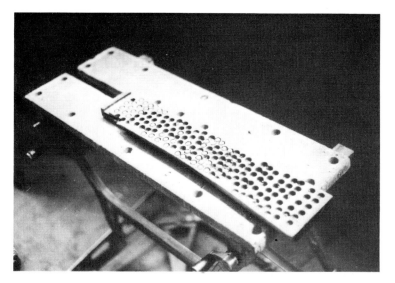

47: Plugs from a piece of scrap timber give a much better finish than filler for screw holes, especially if care is taken to align the grain

now and then to clear the swarf, otherwise it will just clog up, overheat the drill and blunt it, strain the motor and frustrate the operator.

When drilling holes in ply or thin material, too heavy a pressure will cause the drill to burst through and raise a very ragged edge of splinters on the other side. If an offcut of timber can be clamped to the back of the ply where the hole is going to come through this won't happen, and the holes will always be neat. This applies particularly to hole cutters with a pilot drill. The latter acts as a guide to keep the hole cutter central, but to perform this function it must have wood to drill into, so without a backing piece the hole-cutting blade will try to start thrashing around as soon as the pilot drill breaks clear.

Plug-cutting bits are useful little items, which enable you to cut your own plugs, thereby using by otherwise useless scraps of wood, and saving the necessity of buying dowelling which may not be the same colour. It is not easy to use, as there can be no pilot drill, so if not held firmly the cutter will tend to jump around.

Before drilling the hole to be plugged, experiment on some scrap wood to make sure that the plug will fit, either the spade type drills tend to cut oversize or the plug cutter undersize, so a half-inch plug often seems to be a sloppy fit in a half-inch hole. To combat this, grind the spade down a little to decrease its cutting diameter.

Metal cutting drills will be necessary to bore holes in GRP, anything else will blunt almost immediately.

Sanding disc attachments have their uses, but not for finishing jobs. The use of an orbital sander (or an orbital attachment) is the only way to ensure ending up with a flat surface.

Planes
Power planes are available, but at a price. Most home builders make do with one or two hand planes.

The golden rule, as usual, is to keep the blade sharp, and properly adjusted to cut evenly. A smoothing plane should have the corners rounded slightly after sharpening to avoid making tram-lines.

As a smoothing plane is quite short, it will tend to follow the undulations, where present, rather than flatten them. In order to flatten them, a longer tool like a jack or tri-plane will be necessary (*see* Fig. 85). A similar effect, although requiring more time and effort, is gained by wrapping sandpaper around a straight piece of timber.

Planing can be extremely hard work, so stand as comfortably as possible, and have the piece to be worked on well clamped. Like the saw, it only cuts on the pushing stroke, so if the blade is lifted slightly away from the wood on the return stroke the blade will remain sharp for longer. Try not to let the plane slip off the wood by returning it too far. Rhythmic planing is rather hypnotic and it is surprisingly easy to

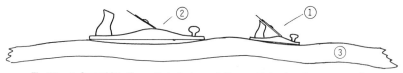

Fig. 85:   1. Smoothing plane   2. Jack plane   3. Uneven timber (much exaggerated)

start on the pushing stroke without realizing in time, thereby bringing the finger in front of the holding knob into sharp and very painful contact with the edge of the wood. It is often easy to identify an over-enthusiastic planer by the flattened knuckle on the left index finger!

Planing across the end grain of any timber tends to break away the end unless you clamp a backing piece behind it (see Fig. 86).

When making spars, or something that is to end up round but starts as a square, draw the circle into the end grain and then plane off the corners; you will now have an eight-sided figure. Now plane off the eight corners and you have something approaching a circle that can be finished by sanding. In this way you keep control of the shape.

All projections left in the course of gluing frames to ply, for instance, can be planed off when cured. This is often much easier than trying to make everything fit perfectly at the time.

Always lay a plane on its side when not in use, especially on abrasive surfaces which may damage the blade.

Be prepared to sharpen the blade frequently during a long smoothing job, it takes very little time with practice and is the only way to get good results.

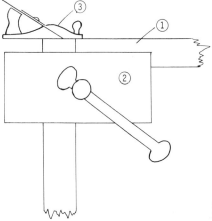

Fig. 86:   1. Backing piece   2. Vice   3. Plane

Take care, with this and all cutting tools, to avoid screws and nails when working.

Screwdrivers

The tip of a screwdriver should be the same shape as the slot in a screw (*see* Fig. 87). It should also be right for the size of screw you are using. This is an often neglected point that frequently results in the tip flying off the screw and damaging the wood, or any fingers that happen to be in the way.

If the tip becomes rounded, grind or file it square as soon as possible. Ill-fitting pump screwdrivers are the worst offenders for scarred woodwork.

Fig. 87: 1. Screwdriver tip   2. Screw head

Mitre block

There are those who can cut a forty-five-degree angle by eye. Unfortunately I am not one of them. A mitre block is therefore the only way I have of ensuring that the corners on capping or frame surrounds fit nicely.

The best type to get have two sides, and preferably metal guides to keep the saw blade straight.

Mallet

This is for use on wooden chisels especially, where a hammer would break up the handle. A mallet is quite easy to make from a twelve- or fourteen-inch offcut of 3″ × 2″ timber, merely by thinning down one end for a handle.

Bevel

Unlike a set square, the bevel has an adjustable blade which can be set at any angle, and so transfer an angle from one item to another for marking.

I don't think any of the other tools need explanation. There are no doubt some omissions, but these may be added when and if a need is found for them.

As parting advice, abuse of your tools affects only you, mostly in the pocket, so keep them dry and use them for their intended purpose. A chisel tip, for instance, is very vulnerable to damage, and although it may be tempting to use it to hack off projections in GRP, it is much better to buy a brick bolster for this sort of rough work, and its edge can be kept sharp with a file.

Tool safety

Most modern power tools are well insulated, but common-sense precautions are still necessary, like not standing in a puddle when using one, keeping your fingers and clothing away from the business end, and wearing goggles when hard, hot lumps of GRP steel or even wood are flying around.

Sufferers of asthma and associated complaints will do well to wear a dust mask when sanding or grinding; in fact, this is good policy for anyone.

As regards power lines, always uncoil them before use, otherwise the 'coil effect' will cause them to overheat and self-destruct. Always keep sight of the lead so you don't inadvertently slice through it or trip over it. When using a plug and socket extension out in the rain, the joint can be efficiently sealed with an old rubber glove with the wire led out through a hole at a finger tip at one end, and the wrist hole at the other. Both holes can then be closed up by taping tight to the wire.

Tool sharpening

It is a mistake to think that very sharp tools are dangerous to use. Obviously care and common sense are necessary, but it is blunt tools that usually cause accidents, the reason being that much more effort is required to work with them, occasionally causing them to 'fly off'. Sharp tools, on the other hand, bite into the timber and do what is asked of them.

The best advice I can give you about sharpening anything, is to restore it to its original shape. All cutting tools have an edge, which eventually gets rounded off by use. The angle of attack is quite critical and may be taken as being correct when it leaves a shop brand new. This applies to drills as well as plane blades, chisels and saws.

This can be well illustrated in the sharpening of a plane blade (*see* Fig. 88), where if the edge were ground too steep it simply wouldn't cut, and if too shallow or tapered, it would be very delicate and the edge would soon break up.

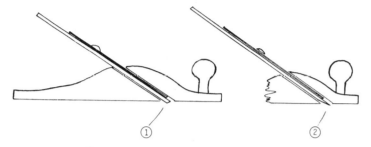

Fig. 88: 1. Angle too steep   2. Angle too shallow

Plane blades and chisels should be sharpened on an oilstone, i.e. a carborundum block, usually with a coarse and a smooth side, and lubricated with oil. If you make a hardwood box for the stone to live in, which virtually consists of two lids so that it can be used either side up, this can be clamped in a vice when in use. It is impossible to keep the blade at a constant angle to the stone if the latter is moving around all the time.

On a badly nicked blade, start the operation off on the coarse side of the stone, using both hands to help maintain the angle. Use the full length and width of the stone to avoid making grooves or hollows. When the edge looks good when held up to the light, turn the blade over, hold it absolutely flat on the stone and give a few more rubs. This should leave you with what is known as a 'wire edge' which is very much as it sounds, and should be rolled off by wiping first one side and then the other on the mound of your palm, with great care to keep the blade leaning so that it can't bite in. If you don't fancy doing it this way, and can get hold of a leather strop of the type used for honing cut-throat razors, this will do just as well.

The next stage is to repeat the process for a few strokes on the fine side of the stone.

This sort of thing is very easy when you know how, a bit like swimming or riding a bike. However, if you find that practice isn't having the desired effect, there are little rollers available that clamp the blade at the right angle. When you get used to it, the whole process need only take a minute or so, unless the blade is really ragged.

If you have a bench grinder it is very tempting to use it for chisels, but if you do, take care not to 'cook' the tip, because this will soften and weaken it. If it turns blue/black, it is too late! To avoid this, keep the blade in contact with the stone for only a couple of seconds at a time, and repeatedly dip it into a cup of water to cool it.

Unless you have a 'saw set' tool and very small files, saw sharpening is best left to the professional, and for drills, a bench grinder is really necessary. They should be held against the wheel with the first two fingers of one hand, while the tail is twisted by the other for about quarter of a revolution. This will sharpen the segment which forms one half of the end, and can then be repeated for the other.

Knives, round chisels or other blades are best sharpened on a small, tapered stone made specially for the purpose. This will help to keep the main stone flat and therefore serviceable for wide blades.

When you re-assemble a plane, hold it upside down with the cutting edge towards you, and eye it up against a light coloured surface. In this way you will be able to see how far it is protruding and adjust it for level.

Buying timber

The amount of timber you need to fit out even a small boat will end up as quite a considerable quantity. For this reason, most timber suppliers will give you a trade discount if you ask for it, which can result in a large saving over a period.

Experience has shown me that it is best to find a good supplier who is prepared to sell to you at a reasonable price and stick with them. In this way you will get good service in obtaining special orders, and they will be more amenable to holding what you want in stock against your requirements.

A certain amount of wastage is inevitable, but this can be kept to a minimum with care. For instance, buying ply in half sheets will cost more than half the price of a whole sheet. Buy framing timber in as long lengths as possible, and sawn timber is a lot cheaper than prepared. It is quite suitable for glassing, being rough and therefore ready-keyed, and a good plane will soon prepare the bits to be smoothed.

Don't be afraid to ask the dealer for advice on different types of timber, and the best grades to buy for your purpose, as well as the most advantageous way to buy it.

Painting and varnishing

The leading manufacturers of marine paints supply booklets which will give you all the advice you need on this subject, and you can do no better than to follow their instructions. This way you will always have the latest information on which primers, undercoats and top coats to use for every material and purpose.

Always bear in mind that the paint only adds a very thin surface gloss to your preparation, so always have everything well rubbed down and dust free before starting.

For a fine finish, always sand with progressively milder paper, and never across the grain, as this will leave scratch marks.

Never apply paint thickly, it will either run or never dry properly. Thin coats adhere better.

Top coats in white gloss are quite translucent, and will show up marks underneath, so if necessary apply another undercoat to ensure good even coverage before applying the top coat.

Clear wood preservative tends to bring out the natural dye in wood. It is advisable, therefore, never to paint straight out of the tin, as the contents will become gradually darker. It is better to pour out small quantities into another container.

Good quality paint rollers are very quick where there is a large area to be covered, and give a good even spread. A hard bristle roller gives quite an interesting 'shot blasted' surface which can look very attractive.

A broomstick can be pushed into hollow-handled rollers, providing good reach, and often saves using ladders.

7 · Windows and portlights

Ready-made windows and portlights are available in nylon, aluminium, brass or stainless steel frames, and in many cases these are supplied as kits, complete with nuts and bolts, gaskets, sealing strips etc.

Apart from hopper type windows, the manufactured varieties are the only ones that can be opened. Many people, therefore, prefer to compromise and have some of each in order to obtain ventilation as well as light.

A purpose-built window or portlight is much easier to fit, normally only requiring the necessary aperture to be cut. Many of them have an interior flange that fits over the inside lining, thereby completing the whole job in one operation. The only expertise required by the fitter is in lining up the apertures, and as a template is normally provided with the kit, or easily made from card, this is just a question of careful measurement.

If you are in doubt as to exactly where you wish any windows to be, cut out dummies from scrap hardboard (or something similar) and stick them in position on the superstructure or wherever. Now stand back from the boat where you can see them in relation to features such as the deck line or the coachroof and see how they look. Most types of adhesive tape will hold the dummies for a while, and this way you will be able to get them just right. It is too late once you have cut the holes!

Normally apertures in the superstructure look better following the line of the deck, but not in every case, and it quickly becomes apparent that in one position they look a lot better than in another. Make sure, though, that internal bulkheads and other fittings will not obstruct use.

The choice of material for the windows is basically between glass and Perspex. The former should always be of the safety type. Perspex is more versatile, inasmuch as it may be bent to a certain extent to match a curved surface, and holes can easily be drilled through it for fastening. It can also be cut, although this is more difficult. A sharp hand saw with fine teeth is better than a power saw which creates too much heat and usually ends up with the blade welded to the Perspex. If possible, order the Perspex ready cut to save problems, and when drilling, do so at a slow speed with a power drill or better still, with a hand drill.

The surface of Perspex is quite soft and easily scratched. Thus windows tend to lose their clarity after a time, and although minor scratches can be polished out with metal polish, it is a long and wearying business. They will stay in good condition much longer if they are cleaned only with fresh water. The salt in salt water is mildly abrasive.

Perspex windows can be fitted in a very basic manner by merely bolting the ply or GRP etc. (*see* Fig. 89 A). But the addition of a flange often helps the appearance. They should be bedded on mastic, and need a fastening about every two and a half to three inches to keep out the water.

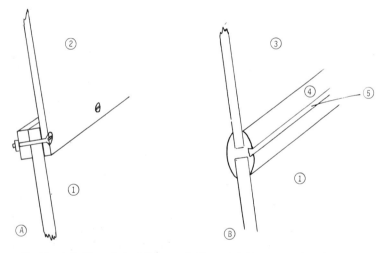

Fig. 89: 1. Hull (coaming)   2. Perspex   3. Glass   4. Rubber surround   5. Channel for decorative bead

Rubber surround similar to the type used in cars is another method where the Perspex slots into one half of an 'H' and the boat material into the other. Both halves are then tightened by the addition of a decorative beading which is forced in its channel by a special tool (*see* Fig. 98 B). The joints are sealed with a suitable liquid sealant the tube of which has a sharp nozzle for access.

When buying this rubber surround make sure the openings in the H will allow the required thickness to be inserted, the metal in a car window surround is only about a millimetre thick, whereas your boat may be three-eighths or more. Worse still in GRP is that the thickness of a cut-out nearly always varies due to overlaps during lay-up. These will often have to be ground flat, otherwise the beading will simply refuse to go in at these points, a thing that can raise the blood pressure quite a lot.

Cutting the apertures for windows is usually quite easily done from the outside using a jigsaw. For GRP a metal cutting blade is about the only type that won't blunt almost immediately, and for ply a fine wood cutting blade will avoid tearing out too many splinters. Err on the small side if at all, more material can always be taken out, but too large a hole may mean insufficient material through which to bolt.

Suitable sealant for windows, vents, skin fittings etc. is a bewildering subject these days, as there are so many types on the market. Seemingly, every time you go into a marine chandlery shop, there are new kinds available, and new methods of application.

To avoid the risk of being out-of-date on the subject, you can either seek advice from the chandler, or write to manufacturers such as Bostik, Expandite, or Dow Chemicals, who will give you the required information.

Basically a waterproofing sealant should remain flexible, so that it is not disturbed by minor movements or vibration. Most are 'putty-like' in consistency, come in different colours (which can help visually) and are available in tubes or cartridges. The latter are cheaper if used in a gun-type dispenser which in itself is inexpensive and very convenient for application.

Some sealants are liquid, and cure on contact with air or moisture. These usually come in a tube with a fine nozzle so that the substance may be squirted into places of otherwise difficult access, such as leaking rubber window surrounds.

Sealers must be treated the same way as adhesives of any kind, inasmuch as all surfaces must be dry and free from oil, grease or dust. In the same way, it doesn't pay to be mean with application. Some wastage is unavoidable, and in most cases the surplus that oozes out as the joint is tightened is not redeemable. The exception is when you are certain the excess contains no grit and is completely clean; it can then be sealed up in polythene or preferably spooned back into a rechargeable cartridge for future use.

Ventilation and trunking

Ventilation is one of the most important and frequently neglected facets of boat completion. An alarming number of craft, even those

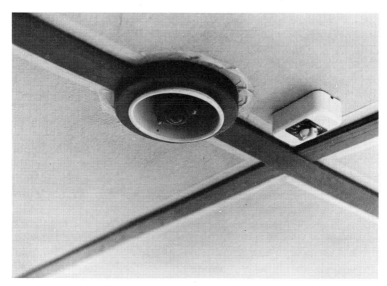

48: Extractor vent built into roof liner battens

49: Where carpet might block off air circulation, a vent in the door will replace it, and is sound policy anyway

with dry bilges, smell damp and musty if they are left for any length of time.

Apart from being unpleasant to return to, this condition is potentially dangerous for the boat and the crew. This stagnant sort of atmosphere creates ideal breeding conditions for fungi, especially when warmed to a tropical humidity by the sun. Fungi is not the only menace; a critical situation could arise if gas or petrol vapour leaks and accumulates in the bilge. Both these substances are heavier than air, and with inefficient ventilation they will sink into the lowest part of the boat and accumulate, sometimes with tragic results. Admittedly there are alarm systems to warn of this sort of situation, but, amazingly, these are installed in a very small proportion of boats.

With a constant flushing of clean air, neither of the above-mentioned situations will be encouraged.

Boats are not at all straightforward to ventilate, because in most cases it has to be done from the top, or at least relatively high up. Also, for security and other reasons it is often inadvisable to leave windows open. Clean air, therefore, has to be sought by a combination of methods.

Hatches with dual-locking positions, louvered doors and windows, and hopper type windows and portholes are all good basic ventilators for the general accommodation. For the bilge area it is necessary to fit trunking leading to preferably more than one deck vent, and these should be of the directional type (*see* Fig. 90) so they may be pointed in different directions to allow the wind to promote extraction and induction.

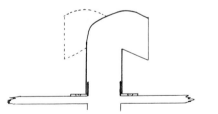

Fig. 90

Vents are obviously very important for the engine-room, galley and head, but the ordinary accommodation should not be neglected. Each compartment should be provided with an opening hatch, skylight or at least two rainproof vents.

Powered extractors are the most efficient of all ventilators, because if foul air is sucked out of any area, clean air is bound to find a way in to replace it. Unfortunately it is only usually possible to use these when someone is around to operate them, and when the engine is running or sufficient battery power is available.

When living aboard, a solid fuel stove gives very good air circulation as it constantly draws in air from the bottom and forces it out of the chimney, making the latter a very efficient extractor. Other stoves with a flue will have the same effect to a greater or lesser extent, and a vent beneath them in the cabin sole will draw up air from the bilge.

Remember that most boat interiors have a lesser cubic capacity than a room in a house, and so moisture and fumes created by gas fires or stoves, boiling water, human breath, cooking etc., must be dealt with that much more efficiently.

8 · Engines

Over the last few years, the small marine diesel engine has virtually ousted the inboard petrol unit from existence.

Although the petrol engine was cheaper, the diesel is much more reliable, especially in potentially damp conditions, more economical and represents a much reduced fire risk.

Petrol engines are now almost exclusively outboards, although inboards are used in inshore or offshore racing boats, where power to weight ratio outweighs other considerations.

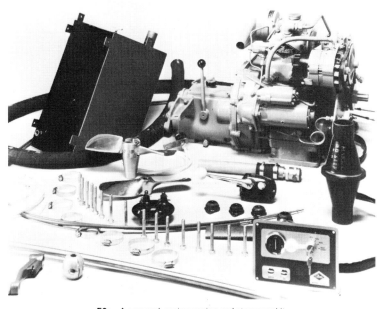

50: A comprehensive engine and sterngear kit

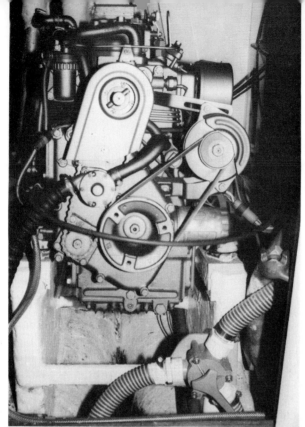

51: Good engine access. View from forward through hatch in main bulkhead beneath companion-way steps

52: Bukh 36-hp diesel with gear-box

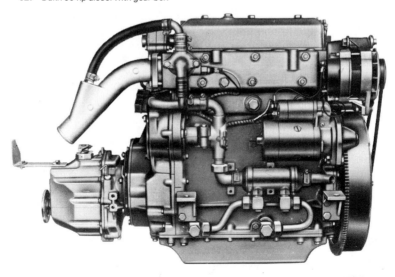

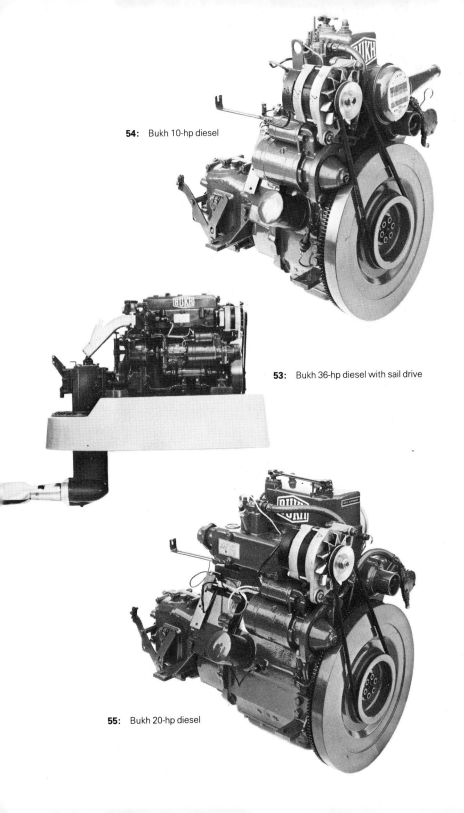

54: Bukh 10-hp diesel

53: Bukh 36-hp diesel with sail drive

55: Bukh 20-hp diesel

There are a few small diesels designed and built specifically as marine units, many others that double for industrial uses such as compressors, generators, fork-lift trucks etc., and a lot that are adaptations of road-going van and lorry engines.

The purpose-built engines are usually more expensive, and should be the best. As usual, you get what you pay for. On the other hand, mass-produced and subsequently marinized engines are used extensively in hire fleets, and seem to give very good service. I think the answer is that diesels in general can take much more work and abuse than their petrol-powered cousins, therefore they are all good, and some are excellent.

The designer of your boat may have had a specific engine in mind, and if so, it will be taken for granted that this is the unit you will use. More often, there will be a choice of a few suitable units, and sometimes it will be entirely up to you (within reason).

If you have a few from which to choose, you will need to know what sort of power is necessary or desirable, and consult with the hull manufacturer or designer. If you are going to marinize your own road-going engine it is still as well to consult the hull manufacturer to make sure it is suitable for the boat—especially if you wish to make a radical alteration. For instance, a motor boat may have a normal installation of two inboard/outboards and you may fancy a single, large engine driving a jet unit.

There may be excellent reasons for wanting the above, like shallow water usage, or for skiing where a jet drive is safer than propellers as far as immersed skiers are concerned, and there may be no reason why it is not feasible, provided it is installed properly. On the other hand, there could be a reason why the hull isn't suitable, or maybe it will need reinforcement.

Another factor with popular boats is that a 'one off' may be difficult to sell.

Transmissions should be treated likewise, but where there is scope for personal choice, the combinations are as follows:

a Conventional inboard/gear-box/stern tube and propshaft
b Conventional inboard/V drive/stern tube and propshaft
c Conventional inboard/outboard drive (Z, etc.)
d Conventional inboard/sail drive
e Conventional inboard/Jet drive
f Conventional inboard/Hydraulic drive
g Outboard

There are pros and cons to each installation, but the choice is often governed by the siting of the engine. In the traditional layout (a) the engine is often almost amidships in small boats, whereas in the cases of (b), (c), and (e) it/they can be located at the stern.

The sail drive is similar in appearance to an outboard leg, but made to go straight down through the hull behind the engine, and with the use of hydraulic drive, the engine can be sited almost anywhere.

So you see, depending on whether you desire the emphasis to be on accommodation, power, seaworthiness or ease of installation, which will again depend on the usage, the choice is considerable—as is the price, so be sure to obtain good advice from the boat or engine manufacturer or both.

For a few comments on suitability of various installations let us go through our list, beginning with:

(a) This conventional layout has one great advantage: the siting of the engine/s is in the best place for the balance of a boat i.e. towards amidships and low down. Because of this, it will always be popular with displacement and semi-displacement sea-going boats where stability in rough conditions is of paramount importance. Propshaft alignment is critical, as misalignment causes vibration, rapid wear of bearings, and leaks. Flexible couplings and mountings are a help here, but should still be carefully aligned. Moving the engine aft to ease accommodation problems can lead to too great an angle of inclination; however, this problem has now been solved by the introduction of the Aquadrive unit (*see* photo 56) which makes it possible to install the engine horizontal, thereby obviating the need for special sumps etc. The engine can also run safely with up to a 16-degree angle between the crankshaft and the propshaft.

(b) The V drive allows engines sited in the stern to drive through propshafts in the same position as they would be for a conventional

56: GKN Aquadrive

layout. The basic idea is to give improved accommodation space, and move the engine noise aft where there is more chance of isolating it from the living area. The stern siting often has the added bonus of greater accessibility, also the engine may be mounted horizontally.

(c) An inboard/outboard unit is literally an inboard engine driving an outboard leg, thereby allowing the reliability of the former to combine with the advantages of the latter i.e. the leg can be wound up or tilted for beaching, weed clearance etc. Installation is also simplified. The engine/s will normally, but not always, be sited in the stern, and special longlegs are available for catamarans where the engine may have to be sited high up. The main disadvantage of this arrangement is that in rough sea conditions, especially following seas, the units occasionally come clear of the water, thereby robbing the boat of steerage until the propeller is able to bite again. On the other hand, they give a boat exceptional manoeuvrability in calm water, making mooring as easy as parking a car.

(d) The sail drive or S drive is a comparatively new development of the inboard/outboard or Z drive. As with the latter, there is no need for a conventional gear-box as this is included in the drive unit, but unlike the Z drive, the leg is designed to go through the bottom of the boat instead of the transom, so the engine can be sited as low as possible. Some makes include a feathering propeller for more efficient sailing.

(e) A jet drive is a reaction unit accelerating water instead of air, as in aircraft. The broad principle is the same, with a deflector shield being lowered to provide reverse thrust and a vertical, swivelling deflector for steerage. The only part that needs to be in water is the inlet pick-up, so a craft can operate in very little depth. Units are available from low power types for runabouts right up to fast cruiser size.

(f) Hydraulic transmission allows the propshaft to be sited conventionally, and the engine wherever convenient. This had proved especially useful for inland hire cruisers, where the accent is on accommodation. In most cases the engine is transversely mounted in a very small compartment across the stern, taking up very little space indeed. The only connection between the engine-driven hydraulic pump and the hydraulic motor driving the propshaft is by three flexible pipes, which is why alignment or distance between the two is irrelevant. There is a relief valve in the system, therefore it is impossible to overload by sudden changes from full ahead to full astern, making it damage proof for inexperienced users.

Some power is lost over conventional shaft drive, but this can be offset economy-wise by the fact that the engine may be set at optimum fuel consumption revs and run continuously at this speed. No acceleration or deceleration is required because the hydraulic motor stores power in the same manner as a battery, being charged by a generator. (g) Efforts have been made over the years to develop a diesel outboard, but usually thwarted by the weight problem. One of the main advantages of the outboard is portability, so above a certain weight this is nullified.

Being transom hung, outboards are very simple to install, and they are a lot more reliable than they used to be, although rather thirsty at high speeds; nevertheless they still hold an important place in many areas of boating, where power to weight ratio or ease of attachment and detachment is needed.

To facilitate the fitting of inboard engines in confined spaces, apart from the normal in-line configuration, other types such as V, or inclined, or even flat units are available, some of which are suitable for turbo-charging for extra performance if required.

Starting is normally by starter motor powered by the batteries. Small diesels may be hand started where swinging space for a handle exists, but the high compression ratio of a diesel confines this activity to muscular gorillas in the medium to large sizes.

Other starting methods include air pumps and hydraulic pumps, some of which are hand cranked, and after the motor has run, will store up enough for the next start. Lucas CAV also make a spring start. All these types help to conserve battery power, which is then available for other things such as lighting, refrigeration, power winches etc.

Marinization

Marinizing your own new or second-hand road-going diesel can save you a lot of money if you (or possibly a friend) have skill in this direction. From the safety angle, however, it must be done properly. Specialized cooling kits are available and regularly advertised in the yachting press, and these firms usually supply everything you will need, such as gear-box, special sumps, adapter plates, engine mountings etc., but the basic idea is to use the cool water on which you are floating to regulate the engine temperature. This can be done in the following ways:

(a) *Direct cooling*

By this method water is drawn through a sea-cock in the hull, run through the water channels in the engine, and expelled through the exhaust or a skinfitting. This is not advisable in salt water unless the engine is designed for it.

(b) *Indirect cooling*

Fresh water is self-contained, and circulated by an impeller through a heat exchanger. The latter contains cooling pipes and operates on a separate system where raw water from outside is drawn in, run through the pipes and then injected into the exhaust system.

(c) *Closed circuit cooling*

As the name implies, fresh water is circulated through a completely self-contained system, usually being cooled by keel coolers (pipes under the boat), or skin tanks, mostly used in steel boats where their construction is simple. These tanks are below the water-line and so, like the keel coolers, are cooled by the outside water.

With a closed circuit system it is quite feasible to fit a calorifier, another type of heat exchanger, to use hot water created by the engine to heat a domestic water supply.

Useful additions to the engine installation are a sump drain pump, and remote control greasers for the propshaft and rudder bearings. The former saves old engine oil from being emptied into the bilge and then mopped up, and the latter means that these two grease points can be operated from a convenient place, and therefore not neglected because they are so awkward to get at.

Sea-cocks for the water inlet to the engine perform a vitally important function. A grill should be fitted outside the inlet to discourage clogging, but it is essential that the cock itself is the type with an integral strainer, as this can be turned off just inside the skin for the strainer to be unblocked while afloat.

Only top quality pipe should be used, and this should be of the reinforced rubber type that cannot become flattened by suction. If more than about two feet is necessary, the majority of the system should be in copper, merely using the rubber for bends (not too sharp) and to absorb engine vibration.

Controls and instruments are usually available from the marinization supplier, and may be cheaper to buy if they are all part of a packagre. Morse/Teleflex cables are easy to fit for most applications, and come with full instructions.

Getting an engine on board

This can sometimes involve the use of a crane, but only a small mobile one will be necessary.

To save the expense of a crane, five scaffolding poles and a chain type hoist will suffice for engines up to half a ton or so (*see* Fig. 91).

'Walking' the poles is quite easy, a foot or so at a time in sequence,

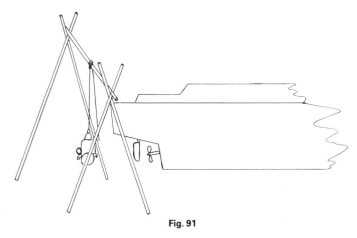

Fig. 91

once the engine is above deck level. Make sure the cross-beam will enable the hoist and engine to clear, and protect the boat against any untoward swings. Scaffolding, clips and hoist are all hirable.

Engine beds

If you know what engine you are getting before you take possession of the hull, the manufacturers will normally put the beds in for you, and if you are sticking to a standard engine they will usually have jigs or templates to enable the job to be done quickly and cheaply. At the same time, they can mark or bore the stern tube hole, and glass in the inboard clamp for the tube where necessary, thus saving anything but minor alignment adjustments later on.

Should you be installing your own beds, some manufacturers will lend or hire you a dummy stern tube and engine jig which will show you exactly where the beds should go; this can be a great help.

When neither of these courses is practical, a drawing from the engine manufacturers of side and plan elevations, drawn to scale with all relevant measurements, will enable you to make up a dummy jig of the mounting feet and crankshaft centrelines (*see* Fig. 92).

The Aquadrive is a boon here, because the height of the beds can be suited to convenience. Otherwise, make the beds slightly on the low side. It is easy to raise an engine for alignment by putting shims or washers under the feet, but lowering it is a major job.

For accurate alignment, the stern tube should be mounted first, and the engine aligned to it. The latter is adjustable by being raised or tilted fore and aft, and sometimes sideways to a small extent depending on the slots in the feet, but the former is fixed.

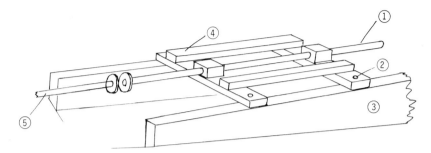

Fig. 92: 1. Crankshaft centreline 2. Engine feet position 3. Engine beds positioned for glassing 4. Jig 5. Propshaft or jig

Having determined the position of the engine feet, measurements can be taken by propping up battens at this height and angle, bearing in mind clearance for the sump, gear-box, bell housing, flywheel etc. and the beds can then be made up and glassed very securely in place.

As the beds need to be upright, the bottom edge may well have to be shaped to fit the boat, and if solid mounting is being used for the engine, it will usually be necessary to bore transverse holes a couple of inches under where the feet will sit so that bolts may be secured (*see* Fig. 93). Flexible mountings will need a depression bored from the top to clear the underside of the mount, and a two-bolt fastening (*see* Fig. 94). Both these jobs are easier to do before the beds are installed.

Another method of securing a mounting bolt is to bore an oversize hole on the 'tooth filling' principle. This can be done by opening up the lower part of the hole with a small chisel (*see* Fig. 94); the hole is then filled with resin, and a well greased, course threaded length of stainless steel studding is inserted and left until the resin has cured. The studding may then be unscrewed, and a neat, threaded hole is left to screw it back into when the engine is bolted down. Needless to say, the holes must be accurately positioned; this can be ensured with the use of dummy engine feet, (*see* Fig. 92) or the complete dummy shaft and engine feet jig you made up to find the engine bed position.

The studs can be unscrewed by locking two nuts (tightening them together) near the top of the inch or so that is left protruding from the beds. Of course, they can be left in position, but great care is needed when installing or removing the engine, not to damage the threads. The diameter of the studs will be governed by the size of the hole in the feet.

It should be stressed that this method, though trouble-free over quite a few years in my experience, is only suitable for engines up to about 45 bhp. For larger units the bolt-through method (*see* Fig. 94 (6)) will probably find more favour with the makers.

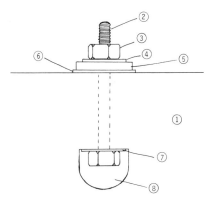

Fig. 93:   1. Engine bed   2. Mounting bolt   3. Nut   4. Washer   5. Engine foot   6. Metal plate   7. Washer   8. Hole through bed

Fig. 94:   1. Engine bed   2. Flexible mounting   3. Securing bolt   4. Transverse hole through bed for access to nut   5. Hole in top of bed for clearance   6. Alternative fastening – course threaded studding, well greased and sunk into resin   7. Engine foot

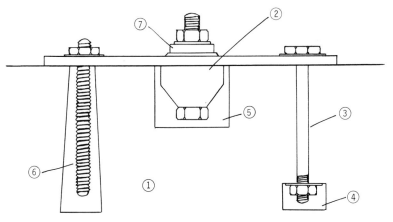

Getting back to the beds, they should be made from two straight-grained, knot-free pieces of softwood such as pine. Where solid mounting is used, softwood can absorb more vibration. Softwood may also be used with flexible mountings, although as the latter will absorb the vibration, there is no disadvantage in using hardwood, apart from the price. In either case they should be well glassed in to become an integral part of the boat. They should be as long as possible, to spread the load, and it is no disadvantage to run the forward end to the nearest bulkhead if a clear run exists, as this adds enormous strength to both.

Where it is impractical to fasten the beds to a bulkhead, cross frames should be bonded in for support (*see* Fig. 95).

The timber, especially for medium and large engines, should be about three inches thick, and have the corners rounded off as usual for glassing. The widest part of most engines is the flywheel housing, and

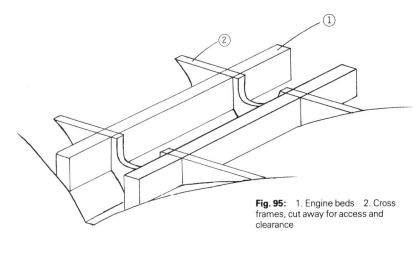

Fig. 95: 1. Engine beds   2. Cross frames, cut away for access and clearance

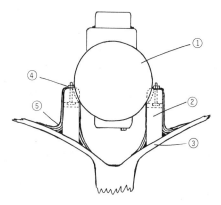

Fig. 96: 1. Engine   2. Engine beds   3. Hull   4. Mounting bolts   5. CSM

wood may need paring away from this portion of the top of each bed to get clearance (*see* Fig. 96).

Engine mounts

Traditionally, engines have been mounted solidly on the beds, and thus robbed of any chance of movement which would create rapid wear in the stern tube bearings.

Although liable to 'twitch' when cold, any such movement is absorbed by the beds, which is why they must be fastened very securely.

With the introduction of smaller engines, which never seem to run as smoothly as their multi-cylinder forbears, flexible mountings can go a long way to absorb vibration which can otherwise become irritating on a long cruise.

As these mounts allow the engine to move, and the propshaft must not, a flexible coupling must also be used in conjunction. Never use flexible mounts with a solid coupling, or the sterngear will be very short-lived.

Although allowing slight movement, the flexible coupling should be aligned just as carefully as the solid type if not more so. As I have found to my cost before now, the effect of dampening the vibration tends to mask inaccurate alignment to some extent, but the bearings still suffer.

Stern tube and propeller-shaft

In the conventional engine layout, a stern tube will be necessary for each propeller-shaft.

Normally made from gunmetal or phosphor-bronze, the tube provides a watertight channel for the shaft to pass through the hull. At the inboard end, special graphite packing and a greasing point form a seal where the shaft passes through the bearing, and the outboard end normally houses a water-lubricated Cutlass bearing, or where the shaft is supported under the hull by an 'A' or 'P' bracket, this will contain a water-lubricated bearing.

The stern tube has to be rigidly mounted to the hull, and how this is done depends on the shape of the hull at the point through which it passes. For instance, where there is a single engine and hollow skeg, the tube will fasten to the flat, aft-facing section of the skeg, and an inboard clamp which can be a well glassed in section of marine ply (*see* Fig. 97).

Where the tube is to pass through a flattish section of the hull, it will pass through a flat plate, which will be part of the tube fabrication (*see* Fig. 98) which will be bolted through, or glassed into the hull, or both.

There will almost certainly be a standard tube arrangement for your hull, or one suited to any modifications you want to make i.e. longer or shorter. If not, many firms make them up to order, and advertise their services in the yachting Press. Fitting instructions are obtainable from the sterngear or hull manufacturers.

Alignment is very important, and propshaft and crankshaft centre-lines should be worked out before fitting. The shaft should be fitted before the engine/s and be in line with the keel centreline. If the shaft (or dummy shaft) is then extended forward, this will be the crank-shaft centreline, or the line of the gear-box flange from which measure-

57: Propshaft bracket containing cutlass bearing and propeller. Single engine installation on centreline

ments can determine the position of the engine feet and thence the beds. If you have chosen a larger than standard engine, and the line means that the top of the engine will foul the cockpit floor, the problem can be solved by using the angled Aquadrive type unit.

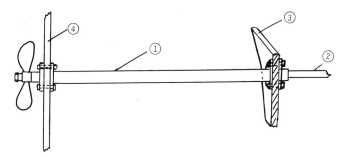

Fig. 97: 1. Stern tube   2. Stern shaft   3. Shaft clamp (half cut away)   4. Skeg

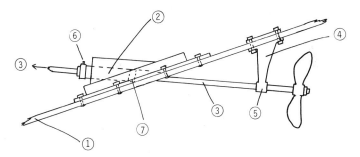

Fig. 98: 1. Hull   2. Stern   3. Stern shaft   4. Outboard bracket   5. Water lubricated bearing   6. Gland   7. Grease seal bearing

Fuel tanks and plumbing

Tanks can be made from mild steel, stainless steel, copper, alloy, GRP or flexible rubber bags as used in aircraft. The latter are useful where a handy space exists to house them, such as hollow bilge-keels etc. (consult with the manufacturers first though, as not all bilge-keels are considered strong enough).

The choice may otherwise be governed by regulations of bodies such as the Thames Conservancy Board or the British Waterways Board, or Lloyds, whose specifications for tanks, piping and couplings must be adhered to.

Special paints are available for the inside of steel tanks, and instructions should be very carefully followed. Large inspection plates for access should be provided for maintenance and cleaning.

There may be a need with some small engines to have gravity feed, in which case tank/s will have to be sited high up, probably under the side decks. Most diesels have lift pumps though, so tanks can be put low down where the weight is needed.

A petrol tank will need three apertures: a filler, a supply pipe and a vent pipe (*see* Fig. 99). Diesels need an additional pipe in the form of an overflow, through which any excess of fuel being delivered to the injector pump is returned to the tank.

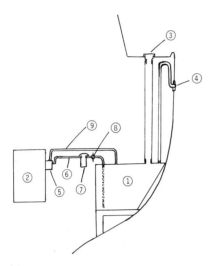

Fig. 99:   1. Fuel tank   2. Engine   3. Fuel filler   4. Vent   5. Fuel pump   6. Supply pipe   7. Water trap filter   8. On - off tap   9. Return pipe (diesels)

The filler should be as large a bore as possible to facilitate fast filling without creating air locks and blow-backs; 2″ internal diameter is a good size. Obviously deck filler and the entry fitting into the tank have to be the same size so that a constant diameter pipe can join the two.

The vent pipe should drain overboard, through a skin fitting, so that in the event of an accidental overfilling of the tank the overflow cannot find its way into the bilges, which could be dangerous at the worst and smelly at best. To stop water entering the vent, it should be looped up under the side decks (*see* Fig. 99 (4)).

The supply pipe will usually be around ¼″ internal diameter unless the engine is very large. Flexible plastic pipes specially designed for use with fuels are perfectly safe and widely used, but if specifications demand seamless copper pipe, give it at least one spiral loop in each section to allow it to flex, otherwise vibration may eventually cause it to 'work harden' and fracture.

The supply pick-up should reach a low point in the tank so that it can pick up the majority of the fuel—not right to the bottom, though, or it may pick up sludge that will accumulate in time. A diesel should never be allowed to run out of fuel, because very few engines have self-priming pumps, and so the injectors have to be 'bled' if this happens.

There should be a shut-off cock on the supply pipe close to the tank, so that the feed may be stopped quickly in the event of fire, and at least one water trap filter before the lift pump (*see* Fig. 99 (7)). Water is heavier than fuel, so any that reaches the filter from condensation in the tank etc. falls to the bottom of the glass container, which may be detached and drained as necessary.

Twin-tank installations may be used individually, a changeover valve switching from one to the other when necessary, or together, in which case a balance pipe will have to run from one to the other from a point low down in each tank. The supply pipe can be made to serve this function with a suitable 'T' piece.

Exhausts and ventilation

Some workboats using raw water cooling or air-cooled engines have a 'dry' exhaust which is often led up above and behind the wheelhouse, but apart from small, air-cooled units, water is generally injected in the exhaust after the gases have passed through the manifold, where it helps with silencing.

Water must not be allowed to run back into the manifold, so unless the pipe is able to run sharply downwards (*see* Fig. 100) the water should be injected into a non-return mixing box (*see* Fig. 101) which is situated well above the outlet point. The latter system is necessary where the engine is sited low down in the hull and the pipe would therefore have to run uphill to the outlet.

The engine manufacturers will specify the diameter of exhaust piping necessary to avoid undue back pressure.

Where a mixer box is used, the dry section of exhaust pipe between this and the manifold will have to include a section of flexible pipe to

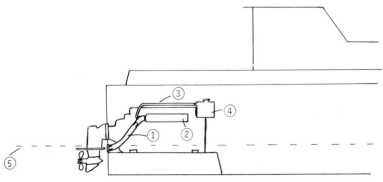

Fig. 100:   1. Exhaust pipe   2. Exhaust manifold   3. Water injection   4. Heat exchanger   5. Water-line

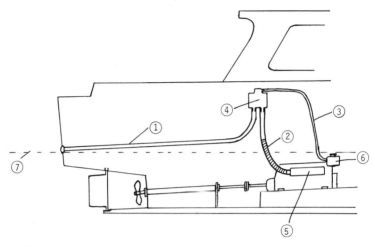

Fig. 101:   1. Wet section (rubber)   2. Dry section including flexible to absorb vibration   3. Water injection   4. Non-return mixer box   5. Exhaust manifold   6. Heat exchanger   7. Water-line

absorb engine vibration, the rest can be made from 'gas barrel'. Elbows, threaded sections and slow bends can be obtained from commercial plumbers or builders' merchants. Armoured rubber hose may be used for the 'wet' section of the exhaust, but it must be the right kind for the job.

It is worth stressing again here, that good engine-room ventilation is most important. A good extractor fan (preferably with a spark-free motor) should be installed, and in addition, two intake vents forward and two outlet vents aft will enable the engine to breathe efficiently and keep the compartment clear of fumes which might otherwise find their way into the accommodation area.

Efficient soundproofing makes conditions on board a lot more civilized, and can be made up with double-skinned panels of alloy on 1″ timber frames and filled with glass wool, or proprietary brands (*see* Appendix).

9 · Electrics

I have always held electricians in considerable awe, and I never cease to be amazed when they read a complex circuit diagram as easily as I can read a book. I remember visiting a new factory in the pre-micro circuitry days, and learning that there was upwards of seventeen miles of wiring behind the computer panels I was looking at. How on earth, I thought, does anyone sort out a fault hidden amongst that vast tangle? Simple, I was told, rather patronizingly, by the genius in charge. All you have to do is isolate each circuit until the culprit is revealed by elimination, then fix or replace the part causing the fault.

What could be easier? Well, quite a lot of things as far as I'm concerned, but he was right. It is very easy to be baffled by the complexities of an installation as a whole, whereas, split up into smaller sections it begins to clarify somewhat.

Bearing this in mind, it becomes possible to work out the various circuits that will be necessary, because on one hand no single circuit must be overloaded, and on the other, there are certain items that need to work independently of others, for reasons of either convenience, emergency or economy. A bilge-pump, for instance, may need to be used at any time of the day or night so you wouldn't link it with the navigation lighting system—or anything else for that matter, but you see what I mean?

How many different circuits depends very much on the size of the boat and the amount of equipment installed, but separations should be planned for the following in an average sized cruiser:

Engine and ancillary equipment
Warning systems (gas alarm etc.)
Navigation lights
Anchor light
Mast floodlights
Internal lighting (a) fluorescent lights
                   (b) filament type

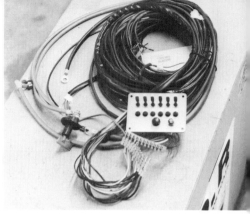

58: (*Above left*) A selection of marine quality lights

59: (*Above*) Wiring loom from Peter Smailes Circuit Marine

60: (*Left*) Through-deck watertight glands and outside light

Ventilation extractor fans
Pressure water system
Bilge-pump
Engine-room lighting

That is already eleven circuits, not counting any sophisticated electronics such as radar, radio telephone etc. and to add to the complications, an automatic bilge-pump fitted with a float switch would have to be left operable while everything else is switched off, even when the boat is left unattended.

Another complexity of wiring for auxiliary sailing craft or motor sailers has been made necessary by the new regulations for navigation lights introduced in mid-1977. Under this rule, craft under 12m LOA

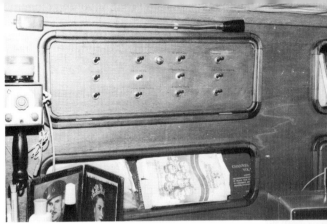

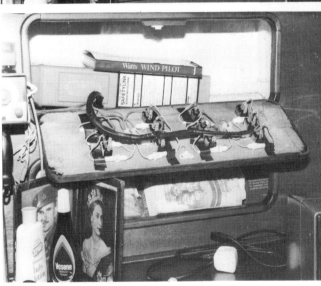

61 & 62: Easily accessible switch panel with cupboard space behind. All apertures have the ply end grain covered with teak, or mahogany etc. Corners are made separately, routered out of solid. Where doors are used, the treatment is the same. (*See also* photo 37.)

(length over-all) under sail need only show a tri-colour lamp at the masthead, but under power, separate port and starboard lights or a bi-colour lamp, white masthead steaming light and a stern light are required.

The advantage of this system is the minimal amount of power used whilst under sail only, but obviously the switching system must ensure that only one system may be in use at a time.

Apart from isolating switches for each internal light, extractor fan etc., to avoid unnecessary consumption, all electrical circuits should emanate from a central control panel or switchboard, with each control clearly labelled.

On small boats, the panel is often on the steering console within easy reach of the engine and batteries, so the main mass of wiring is

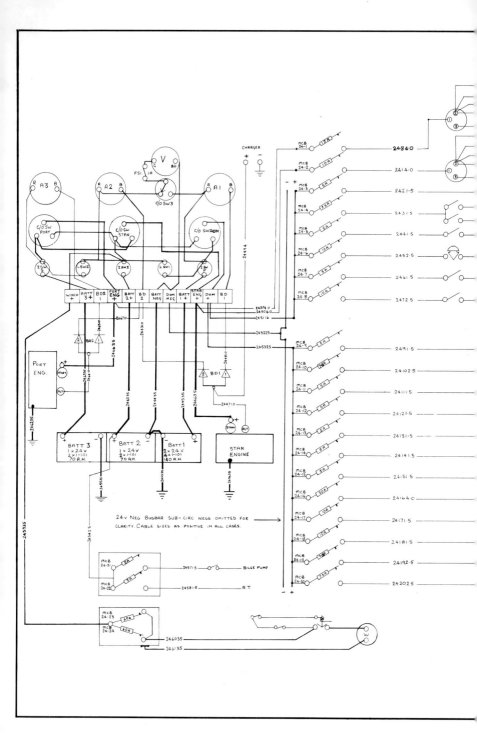

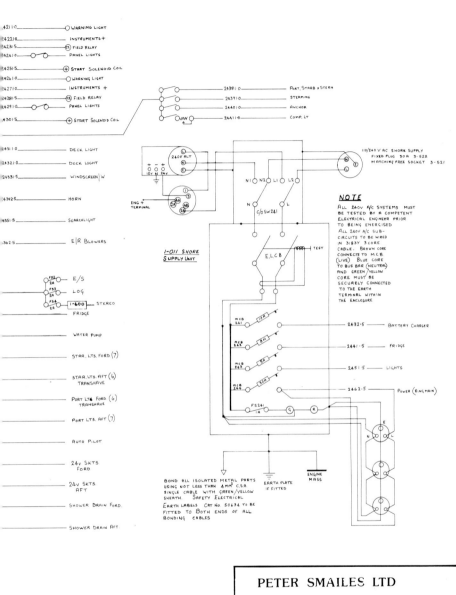

PETER SMAILES LTD		
DATE	9·6·80	ELECTRICAL
DRAWING	206	
JOB No	9940	SCHEMATIC
DRAWN BY	RDS	

clear of the accommodation, and the heavy (expensive) cables are kept as short as possible.

Wherever it is put, the panel must be protected from the elements, especially in a salt-laden atmosphere, and well above the water-line. Good access is essential, so that in the event of trouble all connections and fuses are easy to see and to work on. To ensure this, the panel should be hinged, in which case the wire behind it should have enough slack to allow it to open sufficiently, or have a detachable or hinged door behind it, the other side of the bulkhead.

If it is possible to arrange the access so that you can work in comfort, so much the better, it's not much fun lying on your side in a cramped position while trying to work with small electrical tools, and if you call in an electrician to do it, he'll take longer and so charge more.

Make sure that small fittings that may easily slip through your fingers have a shelf or something to land on before they disappear forever into the bilges.

Marine electrics are probably the biggest source of trouble on a boat. The atmosphere and environment they live and work in is hostile, continually trying to inhibit lasting reliability. The main enemy, corrosion, has everything going for it, and can easily create havoc with a substandard installation in a few short months. This is not, therefore, the place for economy, only marine quality equipment should be used. Tempting though it may be to use car parts because of the price, continual replacement soon makes it a false economy, and if professional help is necessary the costs can mount alarmingly.

By marine quality, I mean the exclusive use of non-corrosive materials, such as salt water resistant alloys, brass, stainless steel, heavy duty plastics, nylon, PVC, Tufnol etc. A lot of cheap fittings have ordinary mild steel parts, or a mixture of metals guaranteed to give early problems. Anyone who keeps a car near salt water will know what I mean.

External switches are available, at a price, and obviously these must be specifically made for the job. Where controls are necessary out in the cockpit it pays to cut a hole, mount a panel behind it, and protect it with a clear Perspex door.

Batteries

Automobile batteries have, it is fair to say, been used for years in boats, and frequently given good service if looked after i.e. kept topped up and given a periodic charge through long lay-ups.

Unfortunately the normal battery is designed for upright operation, so spillage of electrolyte is quite feasible at sea, and is very corrosive. A secure mount and an acid-proof tray are of paramount importance, as well as good access and ventilation to disperse the hydrogen gas given off while charging, and protection of the terminals from any nearby metal objects which could cause a short-circuit.

Battery development has made great strides of late, and special marine units are available that can operate efficiently at 90 degrees without spillage. Another type is filled with a jelly instead of a liquid electrolyte, and is completely sealed, so topping up and ventilation are unnecessary.

Although in units of 12 volts, two batteries can be connected in 'series' to double the voltage to 24, or in 'parallel' where the voltage remains at 12, but the ampere rating is doubled. This rating, 'AH', denotes the number of hours the battery may be discharged at 1 amp.

In greatly simplified terms, volts push amps along a wire, so more volts push harder. As 'voltage drop' is often a problem over a long length or through too small a wire, it follows that 24 volts carry more energy to the 'business end' where it is needed.

Why doesn't everyone use a 24-volt system? Because quite a lot of electric and electronic equipment is only available for 12-volt systems, and the use of a 24-volt system would therefore entail the costly use of inverters to cut down the voltage to certain items. If you ensure that all the engine ancillaries, instruments, lights etc. are made for 24 volts, you will have a more efficient system.

Wiring

When a boat is being built to Lloyds' 100 Al classification, it is essential that 'shipwiring' cable be used throughout. Otherwise, PVC sheathed and insulated cable will suffice.

Each wire, or cable, has a 'current rating' in amps, depending on the diameter of the core, or conductor; it is therefore important that the power requirement for each fitting be known, so that cable with the appropriate 'current rating' is used.

The use of too low a rating will cause a voltage drop, or in extreme cases, a fire, because volts trying hard to push amps through a restricted space become tired and hot. If in doubt, seek advice, and if this is not available use cable of a higher current rating to be safe. A very small voltage drop is inevitable over a long length, but increasing it needlessly is wasteful of power. The battery is drained by the supplied amount of power, even if only a percentage of it reaches the other end of the cable.

Good wiring should be done as neatly as possible, led the shortest practical way between two points, and clipped securely in place. If it has to go through the bilges, it should be protected by PVC or polythene tubing and secured up under the floors where it is unlikely to be accidentally fouled. Rectangular plastic trunking with snap-on lids is useful here, or oval plastic conduit.

Above-floor wiring can be held together nicely in spiral cable wrapping. This has the advantage of expanding to hold any size of bundle, and individual wires can be led out at any point.

A really good installation can look almost artistic in its geometric simplicity, and with the right cable, terminals and protection will last indefinitely. On the other hand, festoons of wire hanging untidily around the boat are a sure recipe for trouble.

Connections

You have probably noticed that there is a loop of wire just before it is attached to a fitting. This serves the dual function of absorbing vibration which could eventually 'work harden' and fracture the core, and allowing some working space during installation or removal. The loop should enter at the bottom forming a drip loop so water can't enter the fitting. Often the loop can be inside or behind the fitting for neatness.

Multi-strand cable should be twisted tightly, preferably with pliers, to ensure consolidation. A light coating of solder will also help, before inserting it into a connection. Too heavy a soldering will produce a weak point where the solder ends which could snap sooner or later.

Crimped terminals of marine grade are quite acceptable if the proper crimping tool is used. This makes possible the use of spade and ring terminals giving easy disconnection for removal of a fitting.

Plastic terminal strips with brass inner fittings are useful when they can be mounted on a board in a dry place and out of harm's way, but otherwise a sealed junction box should be used. Where there is a worry about moisture getting into the box, it can be filled with Plasticine or Henley's compound. This can easily be dug out for access. Any exposed part of a connection should be covered with graphite grease to help guard against corrosion.

Traditionally, all through-deck electrical fittings were achieved by a waterproof plug and socket which screwed tightly together, and had a blanking cap for use when the socket was disconnected. Although these fittings are still available, they are not cheap. Alternatively, a watertight plastic gland can be used, at a fraction of the cost. These have a rubber sealing ring that tightens onto the cable. Slackening of the gland and disconnecting from a junction box just inside the boat still allows easy removal, although it is wise to plug the gland with Plasticine or something similar while it is open, or rain-water could drip through.

Conclusion

I cannot overstress the importance of a good electrical installation for trouble-free cruising. Also, with all the wiring colour coded and a plan showing which is which, any competent electrician can, at a later date, carry out a repair, or make an extension to the system quickly and efficiently.

When the boat has been laid up for the winter and you are impatient to use it in the spring, it is very frustrating having to waste days trying to get everything to function.

It is understandable that some home builders will not wish to tackle electrics themselves, so who is going to? And at what cost?

Firstly, beware the friend who 'knows a bit' about cars and their ancillaries. With the best will in the world this won't qualify him to install marine electrics, which work on different principles. At least ask him to seek advice and equipment from an expert source.

Secondly, a 'one off' installation by a qualified marine electrician is likely to be costly, because a lot of it will be new ground for him.

One economical way out of the problem is to approach a company like Peter Smailes Circuit Marine (*see* Appendix for address) who will supply you with anything from a simplified circuit diagram (an example is shown on pp 168–9) and advice, to the complete installation in kit form. This could include a wiring loom and fittings, so all you have to do is fasten the fittings and make the connections. If yours happens to be a popular production boat for which installation kits have already been produced, this will be reflected in the price.

10 · Instruments

With many new engines, an instrument panel will be provided, and will normally include a tachometer (rev counter), an ammeter or warning light or both, and a water temperature and oil pressure gauge. The latter two are sometimes combined in one unit, each function occupying half the dial. Where hydraulic drive is fitted, a transmission oil pressure gauge will also be needed.

The above will tell you all that it is really necessary to know to judge the general health of the engine and charging equipment. The engine handbook or reference to the makers will give you the necessary information regarding oil pressure and water temperature levels, so if the former drops or the latter rises beyond the recommendations, you will know to switch off immediately and investigate the cause. (*See* section on engine trials, p. 175.)

Instrument freaks can really have fun these days, with extra gauges for battery condition, oil temperature, rudder alignment, engine-running hours etc., many with digital read-outs and most of which can be duplicated for each engine, making a really impressive display. Extra colour can be added with flashing warning lights, many of which are combined with audible sirens or bleepers.

Craft with extensive banks of instruments are normally motor boats or large motorsailers where the engines get a lot of running. Sailing auxiliaries usually rely on simplicity and use the engine as little as possible, regarding complex installations as merely a lot more to go wrong.

Personally, gauges worry me in cars or boats. The smallest fluctuation ruins my peace of mind and has me glued to the dial for the rest of the trip. On the other hand I've known skippers who get endless satisfaction from recording every reading from every dial at least every hour.

As I believe that boating should be enjoyed, additions to the essentials are a matter of personal choice, and money.

11 · Engine trials

Running an engine out of the water is normally damaging. I say normally because in certain cases, i.e. air-cooled units, closed-circuit systems, or others where an adequate water supply can be provided, it can be feasible, as long as the operator knows what he's doing.

Water impeller pumps and water-lubricated shaft bearings will be ruined very quickly if run 'dry', so even if a supply can be fed to the former, the latter should be left uncoupled if you intend to start up.

For the purpose of this section, I will assume that you are in the water, and that at least the engine and fuel installations plus instruments are complete.

If you have just gone into the water, the propshaft coupling should be disconnected and re-checked for alignment. It is quite normal for the boat to alter shape marginally when afloat, which may mean slight adjustments. Checks for horizontal and vertical alignment with feeler gauges should reveal a constant distance between both halves of the coupling at four points, i.e. 3, 6, 9, and 12 o'clock. If this means raising or tilting the engine fore and aft to insert or remove shims (spacers around the engine bolts, under the mounting feet), great care should be taken not to damage the threads. The engine can be raised quite easily, unless it is very large, by lifting one end at a time for shimming. This can be done with a rope from the relevant end tied to the lifting eye provided, or at least to a strong anchorage (e.g. around the gear-box) and fastened to a 3″ × 2″ beam immediately above. Rest one end of the beam on the side of the cockpit, spreading the load if necessary, and get your back under the other while a mate does the shims, and steadies the engine to protect the threads.

Should you feel unable to do the lifting physically, a mini-hoist above the engine with the beam resting on both sides of the cockpit or whatever will do the job just as well, especially if you are alone.

If there is sufficient clearance under the engine it may be possible to raise it with a small bottle-jack, but pads of wood should be above and below to protect the sump and the hull. Personally, I prefer not to use a jack because it is too easy for the raised engine to slip and damage the threads of the mounting bolts. The crankshaft pulley and other projections are also vulnerable.

Having checked and adjusted the coupling, it may now be bolted together.

Before starting up, check the gear-box and engine oil levels with the relevant dip-sticks, and feel under the engine around the sump drain plug to check for leakage.

However obvious this may sound it is as well to be sure, if not, yours won't be the only engine to die at birth because you forgot to add engine oil in the heat of the moment, but this will be cold comfort to you as it seizes up!

Now open the sea-cock (except in closed-circuit and air-cooled units) and check for hose leaks, and check the water level in the fresh water header tank (indirect and closed-circuit systems).

Make sure the stern tube greaser is full, and that some has been injected.

I am presuming that you have a fuel supply. For static trials this can be a clean can full of fuel, held securely in position with the fuel pick-up hosepipe inserted down to a good depth, and secured so it can't slip out. For diesels, the fuel overflow pipe can be led back into the same can.

If the fuel installation is complete, including fuel, turn on the necessary cocks and check for leaks.

Now turn on the battery master switch and operate the starter. In some diesels it will be necessary to 'bleed' each injector while the engine is turning over to rid the system of air. The handbook will give details.

Always have the engine cover or hatch/es wide open when you start up for the first time, so that you can see any oil or water leaks as they happen.

As soon as the engine has fired, check the oil pressure gauge. It might be static for a few seconds while the oil is circulating, but should quickly rise to the required amount.

Incidentally, some engines require full throttle to start up, so throttle back immediately it has fired to avoid over-revving. The checks should be carried out initially at tick over or somewhere near. Never raise the revs on a cold engine.

If the oil pressure needle refuses to register, and there are no nasty knocking noises coming from the engine, try a small 'blip' on the throttle; if this has no effect switch off. Either the oil pressure gauge or the engine oil pump is at fault.

It is difficult to say how many seconds to run the engine with no oil pressure showing. I've known engines that have been standing for a year or so to take a minute or more apparently with no pressure, and then suddenly the needle on the gauge shoots up to 80 psi (pounds per square inch) or so. The criterion is running the main and big end bearings dry. If this happens they will make a heavy knocking that will be heard above the usual diesel clatter; if you hear such a sound, stop the engine just as fast as you can.

In most cases the oil gauge will register after a few seconds. When it has, and there are no obvious leaks, check that water is coming out of the exhaust (this, of course, does not apply to air-cooled and closed-circuit units). It may come out in spurts or fairly constantly depending on the pump.

If all is well, run the engine up to operating temperature (80°–90°C, 175°–195°F). If it stays too cold, either the thermostat is faulty or the sea-cock needs closing slightly, but better too cool than too hot at this stage, so it is probably as well not to adjust the sea-cock until you see what happens during sea trials. If the outside water is very cold, the engine can take ten or fifteen minutes to warm up.

If after about fifteen minutes the water temperature reaches and stays between the prescribed limits, the oil pressure remains constant, and there are no obvious leaks of oil, water, or steam, the engine may be switched off.

It must be borne in mind that a new engine or a newly painted one is bound to smoke a little around the exhaust manifold, where it gets very hot. A new car exhaust does the same, but only for a few minutes.

Oil pressure should remain constant at steady revs; if you raise or lower the revs the pressure will rise or fall accordingly. It is when the pressure drops for no apparent reason you want to start worrying.

After the engine has had a chance to cool, preferably half an hour or so, check the levels again.

The water level in the header tank (closed-circuit and indirect systems) should still be up to the top. If it has dropped, it could be that a previous air-lock has now cleared, or it could be a leak. If there is no sign of the latter, top up again and there should be no further problem.

If the oil level is low, it could be that the filter has filled up, so a further topping up and the level should now remain static. Just to be sure, check again around the sump drain plug or drips under the engine.

Now repeat the first test by running the engine up again, and if the boat is securely moored, bow and stern, and the propshaft coupling is connected, selection of ahead and astern gears can be made, at fairly low revs, to show that the gear controls and gear-box are functioning. Only a few seconds are needed in each gear, and, as the boat may shear about a little, a few extra fenders may be needed.

After you have switched off to check all the levels again, there will very likely be a slight leakage at the stern tube now it has been turned under power for the first time, so a few turns on the greaser will be needed to restore the seal.

Any vibration caused by slight misalignment of the propshaft will probably not show up until sea trials, after which it is often necessary to disconnect the coupling and make the necessary adjustments.

After finishing with the engine, the sea-cock should be closed, especially when the boat is to be left unattended.

As this often means lifting the engine hatch and reaching into awkward places, it is frequently ignored, and most often nothing untoward will happen which encourages future laziness.

Just occasionally a faulty hose or clip will reveal its weakness, and a three-quarter-inch-plus hole near the bottom of the boat can sink it quite quickly, despite the efforts of an automatic bilge-pump.

It is always best to play safe, but do remember to open up the cock again before starting the engine. A checklist mounted on the console is a good idea. For example:

Sea-cock open
Fuel on
Oil level checked
Water level checked
Battery fluid checked
Gear-box oil level checked
Hydraulic oil level checked
etc.

Not all these will apply to every engine, so make a list for your own, in order of convenience, and get into a routine. If you ever loan the boat out, this will help anyone unfamiliar with the set-up.

Never treat a boat like a car. It may be tempting to just start up and go on a nice day, but especially at sea, with a boat powered by engine only, a failure or breakdown could be disastrous.

12 · Gas installation

Propane and butane gas both come under the classification of LPG (liquefied petroleum gas). That LPG can be kept in liquid form, unlike mains gas, means that a lot of power can be stored in a very small (comparatively) container which is easily portable.

Because propane operates at higher pressure, making storage slightly more critical, butane is more popular for marine use, and more generally available in a greater variety of sizes. Although the two are the same in use, each requires a different regulator, so the two types are not interchangeable.

The cylinders are designed for upright storage and use, and it is important to keep them this way so that only the gas content passes through the regulator. Naturally the gas given off by the liquid occupies the upper part of the container, so turned upside down, or horizontal, liquid could enter the piping, with serious consequences.

As the gas is drawn off, the liquid gives off more gas, and the regulator keeps the pressure constant until the liquid runs out.

Apart from the extra weight, it is possible to tell if there is potential power in the cylinder by shaking it. Providing liquid can be heard sloshing about gas is available.

In very cold weather, pressure drops off as soon as the container gets down to around quarter full. To save wastage, insulate it with an old coat, blanket or whatever to keep the frost off, and the last quarter will remain usable.

As LPG is heavier than air, any leakage will fall until it is trapped, where it will collect with lethal intent. In this situation disaster is only as far away as the first spark or naked flame.

There are several things that make this highly unlikely in a good installation, if not impossible. For one thing, a distinctive smell has been added to the gas to make a leakage quickly apparent. Also, there are some very good warning alarm devices on the market which make strident noises as soon as they come into contact with any escaping vapour. These should live in the bilges where the gas will collect. Such devices serve an excellent purpose, but the essence of a good installation is to forestall the occasion when they might be needed. With care, LPG can be used with complete confidence, as has been proved in millions of homes, boats, caravans, mobile campers etc.

Firstly the container should be stored in a sealed and vented compartment, preferably only accessible from the top. Vents should be above the water-line, i.e. the bottom of the compartment should be well above the water-line so that it can be vented overboard. The vents, where the gas locker is remote from the skin, may be piped to skin fittings by copper, steel or approved type flexible hose, of at least half an inch internal diameter for each 15-kg or 32-lb bottle stored.

The regulator should be easily accessible to make changing simple, as should the on-off tap. For sea-going use, the containers should be well secured against the motion of the boat; the easiest way to ensure this is to make the compartment a snug fit. A compartment or protective cage of some kind should still be used if the containers are stored on deck. Elastic shock cord won't hold a container stationary against violent movement, and should not be relied upon.

Thames Water Authority specifications require the compartment to be fabricated from 20 swg steel minimum, with seams welded, brazed or sweated, or a glass fibre moulding at least 3mm or ⅛″ thick made with self-quenching resin.

In the interests of safety, restricted water regulations should be followed even when your only cruising ground is the open sea. You will then not be a hazard to yourself or, just as important, to any other boat moored alongside.

Flexible tubing should conform to BS 3212/1960, and should only be used inside the boat where necessary, i.e. to allow a gimballed stove to swing, or for portable appliances. The hose should originate from a control tap.

It is normal to use flexible tubing to connect the regulator to the container; to use copper pipe here would mean bending it out of the way on each changeover, but the hose should not run outside the vented compartment. The hose fits over a special nozzle which is, preferably, part of a tap, also inside the compartment. From here on, the gas must run through solid drawn copper tubing.

The tubing should always be fastened rigidly, and as high up as possible. Above window height is best, where feasible, but never through the bilges.

Where piping is to pass through an engine compartment, the Thames Water Authority require it to pass through a gas-proof conduit admitting jointless pipe only.

Apart from portable appliances on flexible pipe, all other—cookers, fridges, water heaters etc.—should be rigidly mounted discounting gimballed stoves) to prevent movement from weakening or straining pipe or joints.

As with all types of copper pipe plumbing, the ends must be cut neatly and any rough edges, including the inside, must be filed smooth.

All joints should be made by the approved compression fittings, which may need the addition of 'Calortight' jointing compound, or PTFE tape, to effect a good seal.

The materials mentioned above are all readily available from Gas stockists, who are usually very helpful, able to advise on equipment and fitting, and to inspect your installation, for a fee, to make sure it is safe.

When checking your own installation, a small quantity of liquid detergent on the joints will blow giveaway bubbles if there is a leak. Never test with a match!

Where there is a leak at the cylinder, it is often the small, rubber sealing washer on the regulator. These can be damaged with the spanner tightening regulators by overtightening. It is as well to keep one or two spares.

With any kind of combustion, good ventilation is essential, flames and humans both breathe oxygen, and the efficiency of both can be impaired, eventually to extinction, when they are deprived of it!

Should a serious leak occur, all equipment and naked flames should be immediately switched off, preferably at the bottle (cylinder). Every window, door and lift-up hatch should be opened, and gas collected in the bilge should be extracted.

With a good, spark-proof extractor fan this is not much of a problem, but beware, most electrically driven appliances do spark, and would therefore be quite lethal.

Some people favour flooding the bilge, on the principle that the gas can then be pumped out with the water. Others rely on blowing air in, or otherwise creating sufficient draught to blow the gas out. A gas detector alarm will confirm your success.

With reasonable care, this sort of situation will never happen. Good quality appliances have flame failure devices, which cut off the supply if the pilot light goes out. If no appliances with pilot lights are being used, always turn the supply off at the bottle when not in use, and always have a means of ignition ready when turning on anything to be lit.

Calor Gas Ltd (for address see Appendix) supply installation leaflets and recommendations to comply with Thames Water Authority standards.

Standards for equipping pleasure boats are also available from the British Waterways Board (*see* Appendix for address).

13 · Toilets and plumbing

Marine toilets

Anti-pollution laws in restricted waters have engendered great sophistication in the head or toilet compartment. In many areas it is illegal to use a direct discharge system, or conventional 'sea toilet'.

At the lower end, so to speak, the humble bucket, for so many years the other half of the 'chuck it' system, has been eclipsed by a sleek 1980s version, incorporating a self-contained fresh water flushing system, and a detachable holding tank.

Now that the holding tank portion may be separated from the rest of the unit, this type of toilet is a lot more portable, and much easier to empty than its one-piece predecessor, although the latter still had two advantages over the bucket: it was spill-proof, and hid the contents discreetly.

For sea-going use there is now a good choice of manually operated pump-out toilets on the market that are simple enough to be operated

63 & 64: Toilet, shower, cupboards, work top and sink all in 4' square

by those without a degree in engineering, in most cases, only a few written instructions being necessary.

At the top of the tree, electrically driven models not only take the muscle work out of pumping, but often form part of a sewage treatment system that renders the waste suitable for discharge in some otherwise restricted areas, or retains it in the holding tank for future disposal either out at sea or where a dock or marina discharge point exists.

A holding tank can also be used in conjunction with the manual sea toilet by installing a changeover valve in the outlet pipe so that the waste may be pumped out through the skin fitting or into the tank at choice. In some inland waters, though, this system is not allowed on the grounds that the owner might be tempted to empty surreptitiously the holding tank at an unofficial spot while no one is looking.

As with almost any new purchase, fitting instructions are usually supplied, and should be followed carefully, but as a lot of good second-hand toilets are available, a few tips may help.

Firstly, used models are sometimes quite an attractive buy, because the major manufacturers usually produce a 'perishable spares' set of all the sealing washers and gaskets etc., and short of major damage a quick strip-down and rebuild will produce an 'as new' unit, especially of the diaphragm type. Beware the old-fashioned up and down pump type, though, the bores of the pump may be worn beyond repair.

In most small boats the toilet has to be fitted below the water-line, so both the inlet and discharge pipes should be looped well above water level to prevent any water running back through the non-return valves.

The pipes themselves should be of the reinforced type that cannot kink or be sucked flat by pumping, and should be secured in position by stainless steel hose clips, as should all other pipes, gas, fuel or water. The ordinary steel type will rust quickly and may fail, apart from being very difficult to remove once corroded.

Where a hose is difficult to push over the lip of the stub on the sea-cock, a small amount of washing up liquid will usually lubricate it sufficiently, or better still, put the end of the hose in a saucepan full of hot water, and it will become soft and pliable until it cools again.

The inlet and discharge sea-cocks should be fitted well below the water-line, especially in sailing craft liable to heel over, and preferably sited on different sides of the boat. If this is not practical, the discharge cock should be below and aft of the inlet. Putting them close together may look neat from the inside, and put both on-off taps in one handy spot, but it usually results in pumping back in what you have just pumped out!

These and all other sea-cocks should be made easily accessible, and turned on and off every now and then so that salt and mildew deposits don't seize them up. They are normally left on all the time and so become very stiff, and, apart from hose failure, their ability to be turned off effectively is the only way the toilet can be removed for repair on replacement while afloat.

Some sea-cocks are very ambiguous in their 'on-off' markings. The lever type can cause confusion as to which part of the handle acts as the pointer. They usually move through an arc of 90 degrees, and so although you may have moved the handle towards open, the other end, which is sometimes cast like an arrow, now points to shut! Out of sight out of mind, but the danger comes after you have left the boat afloat for the winter, can't remember whether you shut the cocks or not, and want to remove the unit for overhaul. If you haven't applied red paint for your own coding, test the toilet first, the pump will quickly stiffen if the outlet is shut. Don't overdo it though, or you will build up too much pressure.

The toilet unit should be mounted on a strong, stable platform, and care should be given to its position to achieve comfortable foot room. On a boat with steeply sloping sides, this often involves two steps (*see* Fig. 102).

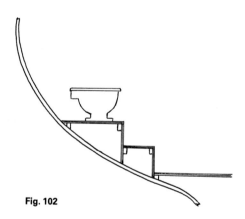

Fig. 102

Holding tanks

The use of a holding tank and deck discharge point can, under certain circumstances, remove the need for an outlet sea-cock altogether. As we have discussed, in some restricted areas this is mandatory, but even sea-going boats spend a lot of time in confined moorings, or dried out on a tidal berth, and a holding tank allows the toilet to remain in use, although a portable supply of fresh water will be necessary when the tide is out.

The size of the tank depends very much on how much you use your boat, the cruising area, and the space available. Where dockside discharge is concerned, the larger your tank the more time you will have between discharges, and in some inland areas, facilities are few and far between.

Fresh water plumbing

Very small cruisers often use a portable container, fitting beneath the sink, with a plastic hose connecting it to a galley pump.

At the other end of the scale, even medium-sized boats are often equipped with shower compartments and hot and cold running water at two or three separate points.

The first thing to consider is the supply. Some boats, whether steel, GRP, ferro-cement or alloy, have tanks built into the hull as a structural part; a tank built this way is able to make maximum use of the available space.

If you specify tank/s to be built in before you take delivery of the hull, make sure that baffles are built in. Apart from the 'hydraulic effect' of surging water causing possible damage, the sound can be irritating when you are trying to sleep on what may be the lid.

An inspection hatch, large enough to see and clean out the inside when necessary, is essential, and tanks with full-height baffles may need a hatch in each compartment. Most hatches can be held securely in position by stainless steel self-tapping screws where 'captured' nuts are impractical. The latter can be welded in steel tanks or glassed into place on GRP, but care should be taken not to mix dissimilar metals as this will cause rapid corrosion. A rubber gasket will keep the hatch watertight.

If you glass your own water tanks into a GRP hull, the inside surface must be coated with gel resin to avoid a plastic taste in the water.

Steel tanks usually last for years with no problem, but may eventually rust and need a special coating. Stainless tanks are very good, and not that expensive, but alloy tanks need scouring and cleaning too often because of the white calcium deposits that form, so are not really practical.

In all cases, tanks should be vented, with the vent pipe looped (*see* Fig. 103 (2)) so that sea water can't get in and contaminate the system.

The deck filling point should be well away from the fuel filler, and clearly marked, for obvious reasons. I have a personal dislike of flush fitting fillers for water or fuel because the dirt that builds up around the edge always falls in when the stopper is unscrewed, and it is difficult to stop dirty deck water from running down into the tank. On the other hand, the raised type of filler (*see* Fig. 103 (4)) is thought by

65: GRP tanks forming an integral part of a hull

66: Tank construction

some to be a hazard on deck for tripping up or toe stubbing. As they are only about ½"–¾" high, I feel this is a small problem, and they can usually be positioned strategically to avoid mishaps.

As with fuel, the larger the inlet the quicker the tank can be filled, and with sound hose fastenings, any excess will flow out of the vent pipe rather than internally, to let you know you are full up.

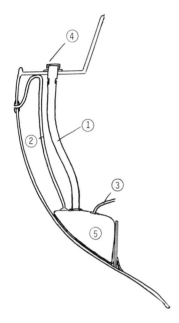

Fig. 103: 1. Filler pipe 2. Vent pipe 3. Supply to engine 4. Raised type screw on deck filler 5. Flexible tank

The size and quantity of tanks depends on the intended use and the ease of refilling. If you intend living on board, then obviously the bigger the better. Flexible bag tanks are very good at fitting into redundant spaces to create extra supply (they can also form a liner to a GRP or metal tank where a foul taste cannot be removed), but mut be of the non-toxic type intended for fresh water.

Ocean cruising experts reckon on allowing at least one and a half gallons per day per person to wash and drink well, although this quantity can be halved by using salt water for cooking, washing up dishes, personal washing and just using fresh water for rinsing etc., once out at sea in 'clean' water. They also favour two or three separate tanks, firstly to keep a check on consumption, and secondly to avoid fouling the whole supply when filling up at dubious sources.

Pressure systems are very extravagant, which is important to remember where supplies are not plentiful. Also, electrical systems are prone to failure, and so a manual pumping back-up should be provided. It would be very frustrating to be dying of thirst with gallons of unreachable water imprisoned beneath the cabin sole.

All hose piping used for fresh water plumbing should be non-toxic and taste free, fastened with stainless steel hose clips, and led where there is no chance of accidental damage by heat or abrasion. Like electric wiring, neatness should be aimed at, with hoses clipped securely to good anchor points, using good radii to avoid kinking, and led by the shortest practical route between two points.

In many cases, domestic copper pipe with either soldered joints or compression fittings can be used, but always ensure that any joint can be made accessible for repair. Vibration can cause fractures and eventual loosening of fittings, and it can be very irksome to have to tear out furniture and sections of lining to find the fault.

All pipes must be cut cleanly, rough edges filed smooth, and where soldered joints are used the outer surface should be burnished bright with hire wool before the flux is painted on and the pipe inserted into the fitting for soldering.

Waterproof shower compartments

Domestic shower trays are often too large for small cruisers, but small ones are available from boat and caravan suppliers. An awkward shape may render even the latter useless, but it is quite easy to mould a GRP tray to fit, and make a platform of wooden slats to stand on to hide any imperfections and create a good, non-slip surface.

Polythene shower curtains tend to cling to you in an irritating and sinister fashion, so it is usually better to arrange the whole compartment in such a way that any splash runs down into the tray, and make sure all surfaces are well sealed with paint, varnish, ceramic tiles etc., with inward opening doors. A hatch or good ventilation above is essential.

If the toilet and shower compartment are one and the same, the latter may be bedded on mastic on a sealed platform. It won't hurt a toilet to get wet.

As it is desirable to have access to all underwater parts of the boat, it is often necessary to make a small hatch in an adjacent bulkhead to enable you to reach the tray. This will also make it possible to get at the drain connection.

The drain itself can lead via an electric pump to a skin fitting, into the bilge for pumping out with the bilge-water, or preferably, in normally dry bilges, into a holding tank for manual pumping out after your shower. With a deep shower tray, and slats to keep your feet out of the dirty water, the holding tank can be unnecessary, and the tray merely pumped out afterwards.

A shower, especially with hot water, is a great luxury, as anyone who has been on a cruise without one can tell you, but if your purse doesn't run to a pressure water system and water heating (and mine has yet to do so) a serviceable alternative is the portable pump-up type shower popular with caravanners. There is no plumbing involved with this type, you simply boil a kettle to make a suitably warm mixture in the plastic container, give a few pumps to create pressure, and turn on the shower head. Admittedly the water comes through in a fine mist rather than a fast stream, but a gallon lasts a surprisingly long time. As the water level drops, the pressure does likewise, and it is sometimes necessary to give a few more pumps, which is no hardship.

This kind of shower is excellent for water economy, and obtainable with a hanging curtain and collapsible tray if necessary, so it is quite feasible to use it in the middle of the saloon with a suitable hook on the deckhead.

All in all, it is much better than nothing, beats standing in the washing up bowl and splashing everything, and provides a good back-up to a failed pressure system.

14 · Steering gear

Most kit form hulls will have a rudder specially made for them and supplied as part of the package or an optional extra. The size and shape will have been designed for the boat, so there won't normally be a choice, except perhaps in material. Rudders are produced in timber, GRP (often hollow and foam-filled), hollow steel, and steel plate.

If you are having one made up to the design, there is often a whole or cutaway section to enable the propshaft to be withdrawn when the rudder is turned sideways, i.e. without removing it.

A transom-hung rudder is the most simple to fix and remove (*see* Fig. 104) as it needs no rudder tube, but where the design calls for a

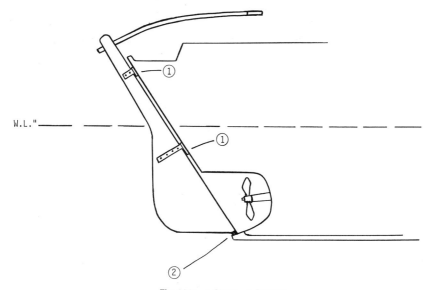

Fig. 104: 1. Pintle   2. Bearing

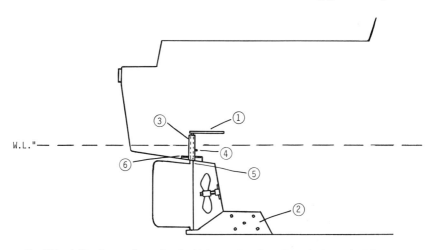

Fig. 105: 1. Steering arm (for push-pull cable) or quadrant (for pulley and wire type)   2. Iron shoe   3. Rudder tube   4. Greaser   5. Gland   6. Steel plate

shaft to go through the hull (*see* Fig. 105) a watertight tube must be installed with a greased gland. (These sort of fittings are made up to order by one or two engineering firms that advertise in the yachting press). As it is liable to be awkward to get at, it is a sound policy to fit a remote greaser, plumbed in to the tube, and attached next to the one for the propshaft. In this way, neither will be neglected.

The tube will be welded into a steel hull, or heavily glassed into GRP. Some types go right up to the aft deck (*see* Fig. 106), and others

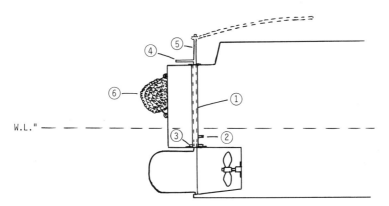

Fig. 106: 1. Rudder tube (welded in)   2. Greaser   3. Gland   4. Quadrant or arm   5. Extended stock for emergency tiller   6. Fender

terminate above the water-line. The latter (*see* Fig. 105) needs the extra support of a steel plate which may be bolted through the hull on a hardwood pad, filled and glassed in, or both.

Where the shaft comes up through the aft deck, a tiller can be fitted, which is the simplest form of steering control and preferred by many sailing people because of the 'feel'. It is also possible to fit a quadrant for cable control (*see* Fig. 106) with an extended stock on which to fit an emergency tiller should the need arise.

Tillers are also widely used on transom-hung rudders, either fitting over the aft deck to the rudder stock, or occasionally through the transom high above the water-line.

Where the shaft terminates internally, quadrant and pulleys can also be used, or it is provided with a short arm to which Morse type cable controls can be connected, or a hydraulic ram, all three of which are controlled from a wheel at the steering position.

Vessels with flying bridges can have a changeover system which allows two different control points, depending on the prevailing weather.

The choice of steering wheels is too vast to discuss here, but runs from the conventional wooden spoke type to huge, pedestal-mounted 'destroyer' type wheels with a built-in binnacle for the compass. A lot of systems, of course, come in a complete package with the wheel included.

The larger the wheel the greater the leverage, and although quite a small one is normally sufficient on a motorboat, sailing sometimes imposes greater strains on the rudder, especially with a badly balanced rig giving a lot of 'weather helm', and so a large one may be desirable.

The latter condition, felt sailing hard to windward, can often be alleviated by fitting a larger foresail and smaller or reefed mainsail.

15 · Deck fittings

Some builders advocate fitting most of the deck equipment at an early stage, so that the ugly bolt ends can be concealed by the inner lining. Others prefer to leave the bolts showing, or at least accessible for attention, repair or replacement.

Having worked on quite a few boats with leaky fittings rendered unreachable by internal furnishings and linings, and having had to remove and replace the latter, I am quite prepared to put up with the sight of a few nuts and bolts for the sake of convenience. Indeed, with a neat and varnished hardwood pad and a bolt of the right length there is no need for too much unsightliness.

Leaks are one of the biggest sources of aggravation on a boat, and many fittings have a strain imposed on them that is bound to create movement eventually. Sooner or later the rain will find a way in, and a quick removal, cleaning, application of fresh mastic and re-bolting will normally cure it provided you can get at everything.

Every outside fitting should be bedded on mastic to form a seal. Enough should be applied to make a surplus squeeze out as you tighten down, leaving no gaps. When a fitting has more than one fastening point, which means nearly everything, bolts should be tightened a little at a time working from one side of the fitting to the other so that the mastic spreads out evenly.

Without hardwood pads underneath, a nut and bolt could be pulled out through the deck if enough strain is put on it; a pad spreads the load between two or more bolts over a wider area.

Where double skinning sandwiches a soft core of balsa or polyurethane foam, it is usually safer to cut the core material out under the fitting, and replace it with a pad (*see* Fig. 107).

Sailing boats will need many extra fittings unnecessary on a motor boat—we shall get to these in a minute—but both need mooring and safety fittings such as cleats, bollards, fair-leads, pulpits, pushpits, guard rails, winches and stem rollers.

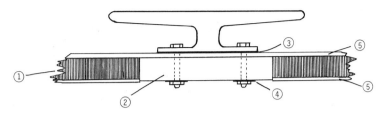

Fig. 107:   1. Balsa or foam sandwich   2. Hardwood pad   3. Mastic   4. Washer   5. GRP

Cleats and bollards are nearly always too small. Any amount of production boats favour small, styled fittings giving a 'yachty' look and about enough room to attach the average clothes-line. Where there is enough material to take a normal mooring line this is usually all, so any boat trying to moor alongside is frequently unable to do so, or ends up tying on to a guard rail, which, being unfit for the strain, becomes loosened and begins to leak!

It's no use saying you don't want anyone alongside anyway, because some crowded harbours in the season make it inevitable. They usually come along in the middle of the night, yelling instructions at one another and ruining your sleep too, but that is another story, and no one promised it would *all* be fun.

Admittedly, large fittings in stainless steel, satin-finished alloy or bronze are very expensive, but galvanized mild steel isn't, and good galvanizing lasts quite a long time. Whether you choose cleats, bollards or samson posts, in addition to one on the foredeck and two at the stern, a further two amidships can be very handy.

The fair-lead is to stop the rope damaging itself or the edge of the boat. Boats afloat are seldom stationary, and the resulting chafe caused by movement can quickly strand a rope or wear through a wooden toe-rail. It should be positioned so that the rope is given a 'fair lead' rather than an acute angle which would soon create a weakness.

Pulpits at the bow and pushpits (or stern pulpits) aft with stanchions and lifelines running between the two make good sense on a heaving deck, although the latter should not be too high, or the increased leverage at the top makes them weak and liable to give way at the base if too heavily leant upon. Boats coming alongside find them ideal to reach out and grab to bring their fifteen tons or so to a halt, so however careful you may be they are bound to be strained every now and then, so choose ones with the largest possible baseplate compatible with the design of the deck and toe-rail. A three- or four-bolt fixing is better than two, as it gives increased strength from all angles.

Anchor winches receive very heavy loading, and this should be well spread by a large and preferably glassed-in pad underneath. Some winches have their own chain pipe to lead the anchor chain below, but if not, or if no winch is being used, it will be necessary to fit one in a convenient position on the foredeck to allow the chain to fall or be piped into the chain locker. The handiest place is often a foot or two back from the stem, and facing aft. This enables the chain to be pulled over the stem roller (which protects the stem), round the winch or samson post or cleat and forward again through the pipe. Having it facing aft also discourages spray and breaking waves from pouring down it.

Sailing boats will usually need a sheet track along either side deck, and a main sheet horse or track athwart, as near as possible under the end of the boom. Both types of track are placed so that jib, genoa and mainsail can be sheeted down in variable positions to obtain the most efficient set of the sail on each tack.

The latter take considerable strain, though possibly not as much as the chain plates, forestay and backstay fittings which support the mast. Traditionally the chain plates used to run several planks down the side of the hull and be through bolted to each one and a large backing pad or frame inside. Nowadays, for neatness, the plate is often fastened internally with a main bulkhead taking the load, and a 'U' bolt or similar fabrication bolted to it through the deck. The chances are that the supplier of your hull will be able to provide you with the right fittings for the boat, but if not, err on the side of strength for the fitting and method of fastening and you shouldn't have any problems.

The mast shoe, or tabernacle, whichever you are using, must be sited as called for in the design, with a suitable pad and support underneath, transferring the load right down to the keel via a post, or bulkhead and post depending on the boat.

With all deck fittings a fair section of the market is orientated towards visual appeal rather than seaworthiness. For inland cruising this can be quite acceptable, but at sea, where a broken stanchion could mean a lost life, or in a harbour gale where a badly designed, inadequate fair-lead could cut through a line and result in large scale damage, good equipment is essential. By all means use stainless steel of the right quality if you can afford it, but ask for assurance that it is marine grade, i.e. EN 58 J, or F, or similar. Some inferior stainless steels pit and rust quite quickly in a salt water environment.

Rather than reduce the size of any fitting for economy, use galvanized mild steel, well protected with paint, which will be a lot cheaper and just as strong.

16 · Masts, spars and rigging

Most modern sailing craft use alloy masts and spars, which are strong, light and drive everybody crazy on windy nights with the terrible clatter made by the halyards flapping against them. This noise, which can do no good to mast or halyard, can be stopped by using elastic shock cord to pull the offending rigging out towards the shrouds—in your boat anyway! As far as everyone else's is concerned, it is necessary to take the same philosophical approach as people living near airports.

68: Rear of engine. 'A' frame fabrication in mild steel sits on engine bearers and supports mizzen-mast

67: Keel to coachroof pillar supporting hardwood mast pad

Spar makers produce their wares for all popular boats, either in a complete package with standing and running rigging, or in kit form for economy.

With a mast kit, the basic extruded section is supplied but you fit the sheaves, tangs, spreader sockets and brackets etc. The majority of these fitting are fastened with pop-rivets, which are supplied with the kit. A gun or set of 'lazy tongs' to 'pop' the rivets is not expensive, but can be hired in any case, and it shouldn't be needed for more than a day or two to complete the job. Detailed instructions are supplied, and careful measurement is necessary.

Aluminium is not difficult to work with, but being soft it tends to clog up jigsaw blades, of which the fine, metal cutting variety should be used. Needless to say, drills and blades need to be very sharp for accurate cutting.

The cheapest way, by far, is to make your own mast and spars out of timber. Until fairly recently nearly all were made this way, either hollow or solid, and gave very good service, in the way that wood does.

Pitch-pine, Douglas fir or Sitka spruce are the most popular timbers and out of these, pitch-pine is the heaviest, and suitable for a solid mast where weight allows, whereas Sitka spruce is the lightest, glues well, and is therefore best for hollow structures. It is also very straight grained and planes easily. Slightly cheaper and heavier than Sitka spruce is Douglas fir. Not quite so suitable but a good substitute.

Solid masts are usually tapered, to decrease weight and windage aloft. Supposing you have a thirty-foot length of 8″ × 8″ delivered, and wish the top to end up 4″ × 4″; the only accurate way of maintaining a constant taper is to cut it first, while it is still square and you have flat sides on which to work. The line can be marked by springing a piece of chalk laden string, pinned at each end, and then pencilled over for clarity. A lot of the backache can be taken out of this operation by hiring a large industrial circular saw to cut away the surplus wood. The cut will have to be made from both sides to get the depth, and there will still be some left in the middle for a hand rip-saw to finish off unless you can get a power saw with at least a 9¼-inch blade.

Having tapered one side of the timber, it will now be necessary to turn it 90 degrees and repeat the process until all four sides are right. With an 8-inch circle drawn at one end, and a 4-inch one at the other, lines can now be drawn to show how much of the corners to cut off; the circular saw, set at 45 degrees, can do this for you (*see* Fig. 108) thus turning a square into eight sides. Careful planing, with much sighting along the spar by eye, will turn this into sixteen sides, by which time it is almost circular and only needs the sixteen corners rounded off and plenty of sanding. Short-cuts on this method invariably produce a dish in the taper on at least one side. By working in sequence, geometrically, a very good circular section can be achieved.

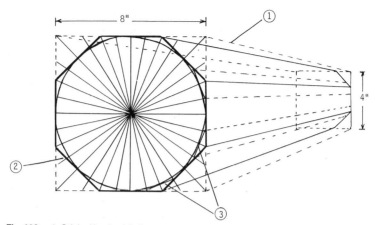

Fig. 108:   1. Original baulk of timber tapered 8″ sq. to 4″ sq.   2. First cuts at 45° to make eight sides   3. Second flats planed to make sixteen sides

Draw in the lines to make all sixteen sides before beginning to cut, it is easier while the end is still square.

Solid booms can either be made the same way, or as a rectangular section of perhaps 4″ or 5″ × 2″, with the corners rounded off.

Pitch-pine is not an easy timber to work with, as the resin content that makes it so durable also clogs up blades fairly quickly.

Sitka spruce, on the other hand, works easily. As a hollow mast is basically a box section with the corners rounded, it is not necessary to have it in one length, and shorter lengths are more easily obtainable. Sections may be scarfed together, using scarfs of at least 12″ in length; these should be staggered so that all the joints are not in the same place around the mast.

A 'scarfing' box is the best way to get the joints accurate and mating up well. This can be made up from pieces of scrap timber, and is merely a trough with two sloping sides the same angle as the joints are to be. Hence if the end to be scarfed is clamped in the trough, it makes an easy guide to plane the spruce parallel (*see* Fig. 109).

In order to keep the mast straight, it will be necessary to have a guide, like a wall, provided it is true, or a series of marker pegs and a length of line.

Hollow masts are usually rectangular in section, for streamlining, and tapered only if required. Solid sections will be necessary where winches, sheaves or other fittings are to be bolted through, such as the tabernacle bolts, and a mast around thirty feet would normally be made up from timber 1¼″ to 1½″ thick, forming a box section of perhaps 9″ × 5″ at the heel, tapering, if desired, to 6″ × 3″ at the truck (*see* Fig. 110) depending on the type of boat and sails.

A really good glue should be used, preferably resorcinol. The solid sections can be added after two sides have been glued together, and apart from strengthening in the way of the fittings mentioned, scarf joints can also be reinforced from the inside by additional lengths of solid, but these don't need to be as long as the scarf.

With really flat and lightly scored surfaces, gluing and clamping should be sufficient, but many builders prefer to use fastenings as well. Bearing in mind that the corners are to be rounded, these should be well buried and plugged (*see* Fig. 110).

The ironwork can be purchased, in stainless or galvanized steel, or a mixture of stainless and Tufnol (for pulley wheels etc.), off the shelf if you plane the mast to suit available fittings, or it can be made up to order by steel fabricators, some of whom advertise their services in the yachting Press. Care should be taken to fasten these fittings with compatible metals to avoid future problems with corrosion.

A varnished wooden mast looks very good when it is new, but better protection is provided by white paint. Due to its reflective qualities the paint greatly reduces the heat penetration of direct sunshine, keeping the temperature and the wood more stable.

Surface tissue and resin sheathing followed by white paint or gel resin gives an extremely tough surface.

Another alternative for economy is to buy a suitable second-hand mast. A lot of owners have changed over from timber to alloy, or opted for a different alloy mast to alter their rig. Some of the prices are very attractive, but seek advice from a knowledgeable source if necessary.

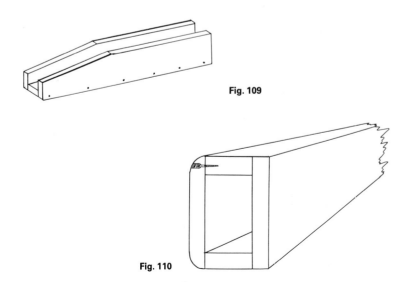

Fig. 109

Fig. 110

Standing and running rigging

As the names imply, standing rigging is that which holds the mast in place, and running rigging hoists and trims the sails by means of halyards and sheets respectively.

Non-boating people are apt to ridicule the many different names that ropes and lines are called by, and dismiss it as 'playing sailors'. In actual fact, although it may seem odd to some, there is no intention to preserve mysteries of ancient tradition. The names are essential as they perform the same function as colour coding on an electric circuit. Faced with a choice of four or five different ropes, a vague instruction to a novice to 'pull on that rope' is nothing like as explicit as 'main halyard', 'jib sheet' or 'topping lift', and neatly separates the rigging from the mooring lines and warps. Hence by learning a few names, an instruction may be acted on immediately and without guesswork.

The subject of different rigs would fill a whole book. In fact, there are a few books specifically devoted to the subject and even these only cover various aspects, showing what a vast and complex subject it is.

Apart from the more exotic but none the less efficient types such as Chinese Junk and Wishbone rigs, two of the most popular are the traditional gaff rig and the modern Bermudian rig. The former, still widely used in heavy displacement boats, has the advantage of a very large sail area, much of which is high up, for pushing power. For lighter displacement and racing boats the triangular Bermudian rig is much more efficient, with far less weight aloft.

These two basic rigs are often, with the addition of an extra mast or more, changed from sloops (single mast) into ketches, yawls and schooners. In the broadest terms, the basic sail plan remains the same, but duplicated. The gaff rig frequently includes a bowsprit to balance the large mainsail with an extra foresail, and thereby becomes a cutter rather than a sloop. Combinations of these rigs make a fascinating subject, but alas, not here.

Taking the traditional gaff rig first, the mast and spars are nearly always solid timber. In larger boats the mainmast, which is quite stout (often a telegraph pole is used) can be supplemented by a topmast on which to set a flying jib and a topsail for extra power in light winds. In rough conditions the topmast can be quickly lowered, but this may entail a crew member going aloft, a sort of masochistic fun. The mainsail is controlled by a yard or gaff along the top edge, running from the mast to the peak of the sail. Having four corners to control the running rigging is fairly complex at first, and it is wise to build a cleat horse at the bottom of the mast to hold all the halyards.

Being essentially a heavy rig, it is normal to use galvanized plough steel standing rigging and mild steel (also galvanized) fittings and bottle screws. It would take a wealthy man indeed to afford the latter in stainless! Boiled linseed oil will keep the stays in good shape for years.

Even some traditionalists now use man-made fibre for sails and running rigging. Canvas sails can be absolute purgatory to handle in cold, wet weather, when the various anti-rot and mildew treatments make them more like stiff cardboard, and hemp ropes kink and knot infuriatingly. Modern science has to have *some* advantages.

The mainsail (and its smaller counterpart the mizzen, if any) is either laced to the mast or attached by hoops to facilitate raising and lowering, and the gaff and boom have jaws which fork around the mast with a line tied across the two ends to entrap them.

The gaff rig may sound complex, and to some extent it is, although it can be simplified a little by the use of modern winches etc. Nevertheless, earlier this century a 'man and boy', the latter often denoting junior rank rather than age, used to manage fishing smacks, pilot cutters and luggers on unpolluted seas between the two of them, showing that the rig, when mastered, is just as handy as any other.

The Bermudian rig suits the modern, light displacement craft very well, and is light and easy to handle. The mainsail slides up the mast in a track and the same way along the boom. Modern development of roller and furling reefing methods have greatly reduced the backache of reducing the sail area in rough weather. Large genoas and spinnakers make for fast sailing even in light winds, and all sails are light and easy to handle.

A single halyard only is required for each sail, cutting down on running rigging, and smaller and lighter bottle or rigging screws can be used, making stainless steel more feasible.

The mast is usually quite tall compared with the gaff rig, and will therefore need one or more sets of spreaders for support, as well as the normal shrouds (upper and lower athwart stays).

Both standing and running rigging can be bought cheaper by the roll, so standardization is an advantage. Spare lengths are always useful, but much of the surplus can be utilized as lifelines, guard rails and mooring lines.

Eye-splicing of wire rigging is rare these days, having been superseded by Talurit splicing and Norseman terminals, the former operated by a local agent is a portable machine, and the latter is a good DIY method.

Running rigging will need eye-splices for the shackles to fit on to and although these can be made up to order, there are some good books on the subject of knots and splices to enable the home builder to do his or her own.

Any rigging is only as strong as the connecting shackle, so these should be adequate for the job.

There are standard sails available for most popular boats, but 'one offs' can be made to order. Naturally the former is cheaper.

Wealthy racing yachtsmen sometimes discard old sails like old socks, and in this sport 'old' often means a season—in other words, 'as new' to a lot of us. Many of these and others find their way to the second-hand market and often make a good buy. It can be cheaper to have modifications made than to buy a new sail, although many are suitable already. The mainsail of a popular dinghy, for example, made a perfectly good topsail on a gaff cutter I once owned.

Large savings are possible this way, but like all other departments, make sure what you are buying is good, or at least repairable.

17 · Cosmetics and launching

For some reason unknown to me, rumour has it that it is bad luck to lay a keel or launch a boat on a Friday!

Armed with this invaluable piece of information, you can now start making plans to contact the crane-hire company with a view to dropping your creation into its natural environment, but more about this later, there are some final preparations to execute first.

A good quality marine anti-fouling paint is said not to poison all the fish for miles around, but it does discourage marine growth from attaching itself to the underwater section of your boat.

On inland water, where speed is restricted, this is not so much of a problem, and in any case, in many areas, the weed can be brushed off the sides, and the bottom will self-clean on the mud.

The mixture of weed and barnacles found in salt water is extremely adhesive, and a good growth will take knots off the speed of any boat, power or sail.

Barnacles love GRP. Not content with sticking to the surface they seem to burrow into it, so that when you scrape them off half the gelcoat comes off as well.

To prevent this, a boat of any material must have a good coat of anti-fouling at least once a year, especially if it is laid up afloat for long periods. Static boats put the odds in favour of the growth, although in tropical waters, offshore high-speed barnacles seem to have no difficulty in establishing territory on the underside of boats doing a steady five knots—ask any ocean sailor!

All materials need a painting 'system' to ensure sound application. Surfaces must be clean and grease-free, and the weather must be kept at bay. GRP and alloy need special etching primers which prepare the surface for the following coat, which must be applied within a certain time (10 hours maximum for alloy). Details for all kinds of paint systems are given in comprehensive booklets issued by the major paint companies (*see* Appendix for addresses); advice and instructions should be followed studiously for good results.

GRP hulls will be self-coloured, so having masked off, separately, the water-line and boottopping, pull the masking tape off as soon as possible after painting (otherwise it's almost as bad as barnacles). The topsides should be well wax polished for protection.

Masking off for the boottopping stripe is a 'catch 22' situation if you are in a hurry, because masking tape applied to non-hardened paint will pull some of it off when removed. I have yet to find an answer to this problem, and rely on touching up the bare patches afterwards. Of course, with more time it sometimes doesn't happen, but some anti-fouling paints lose their potency if not put in the water within a certain time.

If you have a deep-keeled boat, and no local wharf against which to lean it every now and then, or if beaching is impractical in your area, future access to the bottom can be expensive, entailing cranes or gantry hoists. Bearing this in mind, it really is worth doing a good job, and when the boat is dangling during the craning operation, have some anti-fouling paint and a brush handy to touch up any parts you were unable to reach when it was on the ground.

Being highly toxic, as underwater paint has to be to achieve its object, the skin should be protected while painting. Long-handled rollers can save you lying underneath and getting dripped on, but care should still be taken. A good barrier cream will help, and protective gloves, whatever the weather. Having said this, I have to admit that my skin, unaffected by almost everything else, comes out in tiny spots every time I do it, which is as seldom as I can get away with. Nasty stuff, but very necessary at sea.

I feel I covered craning well enough at the other end of this book, but there are one or two further points I would like to mention. Have spreaders ready to keep the strops away from the new topside paint or varnish work. Check the all-up weight if the crane has a gauge. Don't forget to leave fore and aft ropes dangling to check untoward swinging, and in the case sailing boats, if you intend to keep the crane on to raise the mast, and this is the easiest way to do it, tie four guy-ropes to the top so that if the stays need modification before they will fit, you can secure the mast and dispense with the crane. The guy-ropes can be untied later either by using a ladder (well secured), or by going up in a bosun's chair shackled to a halyard.

Mast winches will help wind a body up the mast, but without them you may well need two people pulling, while you take some of the strain by pulling yourself up on the shrouds, if you can reach them, or another, well secured, halyard. Permanent steps or the hoist-up type are a great aid to mast climbing.

In a lot of cases the crane strops will damage the boottopping paint and possibly smear it up the topsides, so one of the first jobs in the water will be to clean off any smears with turpentine or thinners, touch up the paint, and re-polish the hull where necessary. A dinghy or raft will help reach these spots.

A word of warning. As soon as you are in the water, before the crane strops are removed, spend a few minutes checking for leaks. This will be your first chance to test the seal of all the underwater fittings. Leaks, apart from maybe sternshaft and rudder glands where the greasing may have been insufficient, don't cure themselves, so you may have to be lifted back out for a short while to do some quick dismantling, cleaning and re-sealing with mastic. Two pairs of hands, one outside and one in, are sometimes essential here, so line up the help before the crane comes.

Otherwise, good luck and safe sailing. You've earned it!

18 · Practical matters

Moorings

Even with the growth of modern marinas the mooring situation has been outpaced by the number of boats in some areas. If you live in one of these, it is wise to start hunting for a mooring well before launching time.

While saying this, it is quite apparent that many yachtsmen approach this problem in a direct manner, and simply sail into a harbour, drop anchor, and call it home.

Sometimes this pays off, and nothing seems to come of it, but this will mostly apply to quiet river estuaries and saltings (mud flats) that dry out between tides, so the boat should be capable of taking the ground and standing up. Nice, convenient moorings take negotiation and forward planning.

Insurance

Plenty of good insurance companies advertise in the yachting Press, and as a boat represents a very large investment for most of us, this sort of protection is common sense.

While you are building, it is normal to have a special builder's policy. This should cover the boat from the day of delivery up to launching, and include transport and crane accidents. It will increase steadily in value to keep pace with such additions as engines etc., and the building programme.

Once in the water, the policy will depend on your cruising area and locality.

Registration

Lloyds registration, for a small fee, will include your boat and its salient details in the next issue of Lloyds Register of Yachts. For an additional sum, Lloyds will present you with the relevant copy of the register with the name of your boat embossed on the cover.

To give you any sort of rights when going abroad, British Registration is necessary. In fact many countries now insist on it. The registration will provide the boat with official documentation and proof of ownership. It will also involve a measurement survey which concerns cubic capacity and allowances for various compartments such as engine-rooms, chart space etc., all of which means very little to a private pleasure craft, but it is necessary anyway. Details and the pertinent forms are available from the local port authority, who will also normally take care of the survey, or advise who will, i.e. The RYA (Royal Yachting Association) etc. Apart from this, you will be required to pay a fee, and the boat will be issued with an offficial number and a tonnage in units and hundredths, which must be carved into a non-removable part of the internal structure. It used to be the main beam, but very few boats have these nowadays, so a bulkhead or a plaque glued to one has to do.

Most ports have their own registration so that they can charge you harbour dues, and for inland waters it will be necessary to register with the relevant authority, such as the British Waterways Board or the Thames Conservancy etc.

19 · Care and maintenance

It may seem a bit early to start talking about this subject, but it is surprising how quickly the condition of a boat deteriorates if it isn't looked after.

Apart from a naturally hostile environment created by the proximity to water, flying debris kicked up by passing traffic, unburned fuel from aircraft, and muck from nearby power station chimneys are some of the things that stain paintwork and GRP.

Twice a year wax polishing will help GRP to survive the onslaught and a proprietary cleaning compound used first will remove most marks.

For ordinary paintwork regular washing with a strong detergent and rinsing with fresh water usually does the trick.

Damaged paint should be repaired quickly, or moisture will creep underneath and begin to make the situation worse. This is especially so where the alteration in temperature and humidity causes wood to expand or contract and breaks the paint line over a joint. By paint, I also include varnish, and here the evidence of neglect will soon show itself by a greying in the surrounding woodwork.

Once the problem reaches this stage, revarnishing will not bring the colour back, it will only seal the grey permanently in place.

This can be a problem with plywood, because the outside veneer is very thin, and vigorous rubbing down will go clean through it and ruin the look of this area for ever, unless paint is used instead of varnish to cover it up. The trick is to strip the surrounding varnish with a normal paint stripper, and apply a bleaching agent to the grey wood. There is one proprietary brand called 'Colorback' which works well, but it is not always widely available. In this case, a small quantity of oxalic acid crystals sold by most chemists very cheaply (they might ask you what you want it for), stirred up in warm water and rubbed into the affected area with a rag will do just as well. Those with sensitive skin should wear gloves, although it is a very mild solution. Wear a dust mask when sanding a large area with a power sander, as breathing in the dust usually results in violent coughing fits.

Having treated the area and restored the colour, the gap, joint, shake (longitudinal split in solid spars) or whatever should be filled with waterproof filler and revarnished (try to match the colour of the filler, as near as possible to the timber).

Caught quickly, the greying doesn't have time to spread or penetrate very far, but left over a winter's lay-up the damage can become irretrievable.

Paint and varnish should never be allowed to become too thick, or it loses flexibility and cracks or chips very easily. Rubbing down in-between coats or before repainting prevents this, and prepares the surface for the next coat. Remember, if you are going to use varnish, always rub with the grain, or the surface scratches will show.

If metal parts rust, they should be burnished back to a clean surface, treated with a cold galvanizing paint or rust-proofing agent, and repainted. If the rust recurs consistently in the same spot, it is very likely to be some form of electrolytic action caused by the pairing of dissimilar metals, and should be rectified; rust stains that are allowed to establish themselves over a period are very difficult to remove.

Any pitting in poor quality stainless steel can usually be removed with metal polish or chrome cleaner.

20 · Anchors

In the event of engine failure, the anchor is the only chance of stopping a runaway or drifting boat, and if the direction of drift is towards a hazard it becomes an essential piece of equipment.

Anchoring is a very important safety aspect of boating, and the techniques, described in practical yachting books and magazines, should be well studied.

The development in the design of anchors produces new models every now and then, and the makers provide tables showing the right size to buy for boats of different lengths and tonnages. If in doubt, it is safer to go up in size, especially if your boat has a lot of windage or an underwater configuration prone to being gripped by currents.

Even if you intend to use rope instead of chain, a couple of fathoms of chain attached to the anchor will help it to lie flat and get a grip. The amount of chain or rope paid out should be at least three times the depth of water to be effective.

The best place for an anchor is a self-stowing position where it automatically locks itself into place; this can be arranged with some of the more recent designs of the last fifty years, such as the Danforth, CQR or Plough, and the Bruce. With these, the shaft can be pulled over the stem roller, and the flukes, hanging or facing down, depending on the type, jam up neatly against the reinforcement provided (never against GRP).

Where the anchor is to be laid on deck, chocks should be provided to hold it safely in place. The cord securing it should be simple but strong, and easy to undo quickly.

21 · Luxury afloat

Spartan living is an almost accepted part of small boat cruising. The luxury of showers, hot and cold running water, ducted heating etc., has been the province of the wealthy and conjures up mental pictures of Riviera harbours and crew in blue blazers and white trousers.

This is not so today; modern science in combination with industries never slow to recognize opportunities, has come up with numerous aids to comfort suitable for the smallest of cruisers. Some at quite reasonable prices too.

Of course, a lot of yachtsmen find 'roughing it' all part of the allure, or prefer utter simplicity in their boats in the quest for reliability, and there is something to be said for both these attitudes.

Personally, I am forcibly reminded of one two-week cruise in a thirty-footer involving two couples. This was South Coast cruising in the summer. The weather from the start was cold, windy and very wet. Clothes that get soaked with salt water never dry out properly and soon feel very uncomfortable. Lighting the gas oven gave heat, but also raised the humidity level to a point where anything not already damp quickly became so. In a word; misery.

Cruising should be fun!

Not everyone can spend time in the Mediterranean or the West Indies, and local cruising is always, to put it kindly, a bit chancy weatherwise. Moreover, a few home comforts can greatly extend the season even into the winter, allowing the boat owner to get maximum value for money on the investment, and regular use is better for equipment and machinery than neglect.

To start off with heating, it is of paramount importance to remember that good ventilation must form part of an efficient system, a very vital part. The oxygen any heater uses must be replaced. Without it, the ensuing suffocation combined with carbon monoxide fumes can be highly dangerous—this has, in fact, been the cause of many tragedies. Poor ventilation will cause headaches and drowsiness—no ventilation will cause death!

It is vitally important, whatever the weather, to leave ventilators and preferably some windows or portholes open while cooking or if a heater is on. This may cause a draught, although this can often be minimized by opening those on the sheltered side.

Extraction is the most efficient and comfortable means of creating a circulation. If you suck air out, fresh air will find a way in. If you blow fresh air in the result is usually a draught.

Portable or fixed LPG heaters, especially the catalytic (no flame) type, produce a lot of heat, but no circulation. An extractor fan or a vent above will help, in conjunction with other openings (ports etc.).

Small, fixed heaters with sealed flues, burning oil, LPG or charcoal are very good for small cabins, as most of the fumes are automatically extracted, and the circulation created draws in fresh air. This type is normally safe for use at sea.

A solid fuel wood- or coal-burning stove of the proper type, firmly mounted, will often provide hot water as well as ample warmth. The air circulation is efficient to a degree that sometimes produces a cold draught at foot level. One way of turning this suction to good effect is to put a grating in front and just beneath, through to the bilges; thus this often neglected area will be kept freshened by constant changes of air.

69 & 70:   Space is found for a heater; handhold pillars also stop the hot flue being grabbed

With all flue type heaters, the pipe may be led up through a cupboard which becomes ideal for storing warm, dry clothes. Make sure though, that neither clothes nor timber are able to touch the flue, which gets very hot. For the same reason, a proper deck fitting must be used if the deck is GRP or timber. This will have a collar that allows an air gap around the pipe.

For larger yachts and inland cruisers, a solid fuel stove with a water heating facility, a drip feed oil or an LPG boiler can form part of a central heating system using domestic type radiators.

Ducted hot air heaters can produce good, dry heat, although no extraction. These are usually powered by LPG to provide the combustion and an electric fan to blow the resulting heat through trunking into one or more compartments. The units are quite small, fitting into confined spaces quite easily, and require a deck fitting for the exhaust. I mention the latter, because it is often a spring-loaded fitting that can be closed off almost flush when the heater is not in use to save impeding the deck area unnecessarily. It is very important to remember to open the flue fitting before ignition.

By the use of a calorifier, which is a very efficient form of domestic hot water tank, heat can be readily obtained from a water-cooled engine. Normally the heat created by circulating water around an engine is wasted. If a calorifier is included in the system the hot water runs through a coiled pipe inside, heating the stored water in the same manner as a domestic immersion heater. This can then be drawn off as required. Some calorifiers are also fitted with an immersion heater boss thus providing an alternative heat source where mains electricity is available.

To give some idea of the heat normally wasted while under power, the Coburn type of calorifier will have twelve gallons of very hot water ready for use after a 1000-cc engine has been running for thirty minutes! Moreover, the cylinders are so well insulated that water will keep hot for hours after the engine has been switched off.

The above will be used as part of a pressure system, and is installed between the pump and hot water outlets.

A popular heat source for a pressure system is the LPG wall-mounted heater. The advantages of this type are instant hot water at the turn of a tap, and the ability to provide it constantly independent of any other back-up, for showers and washing up, etc.

Nearly all these items are suitable for DIY fitment provided instructions are followed and normal care is taken.

Pressure water systems are available for all sizes of boat, and designed to supply one or more outlets depending on the size and power of the pump.

The pressurized water is contained in a tank and controlled by cut-in and cut-off switches. Turning on any tap in the system i.e.

shower, sink tap etc., will eventually lower the pressure to the cut-in point at which time the pump will be activated until the pressure reaches the cut-off level.

Although a lot of pumps are built to withstand dry running, it is as well to keep the supply tank/s topped up. A great deal of water can be used very easily, and it is surprising how quickly you can run out.

In the event of a breakdown to the system, it is always as well to install at least one hand-pump outlet direct to the main tank.

22 · Electrolytic action

Dissimilar metals immersed in sea water act rather like an accumulator, and in grealy simplified terms this means that the electrical current produced will cause one metal to be sacrificed when in proximity to another of different potential, causing rapid corrosion and sometimes eventual disappearance of the lesser metal.

The most effective way of eliminating this problem is to fit sacrificial anodes. These, as their name implies, will become the target of any corrosion in conditions where electrolytic action is present, and allow essential parts such as propellers, stern shafts and tubes, rudders etc., to carry on their function unscathed.

In the course of their duty, anodes don't last for ever, and should be checked whenever the boat is out of the water, and renewed if necessary.

Internal wiring connecting propshafts, bronze sea-cocks etc. to the anodes is usually recommended, but this varies with different installations. Recommendations will often be given with stern tube and engine purchases, but if in doubt, M. G. Duff Ltd (see Appendix for address) have become experts in this field and supply all the necessary materials and advice.

23 · Variations for steel and ferro-cement hulls

Apart from the fact that deck fittings, stern tube, rudder tube etc., can all be welded to a steel hull, obviating the need for holes through which to bolt everything, the essential part of fitting out the interior of a steel, GRP or ferro is very similar, varying only in the method of attaching bulkheads and furniture to the hull.

Steel boats don't all have steel bulkheads, and those that do often only have one or two, to divide the boat into definite watertight compartments. Some are provided with bulkheads only up to floor level, and the intention is to do the rest in timber.

Both steel and ferro hulls tend to be very rigid by virtue of their construction, and in a lot of cases bulkheads are merely added as a method of division rather than a vital structural member, and so where no obvious anchor points exist it is possible to attach minor bulkheads straight onto the lining (*see* Fig. 111).

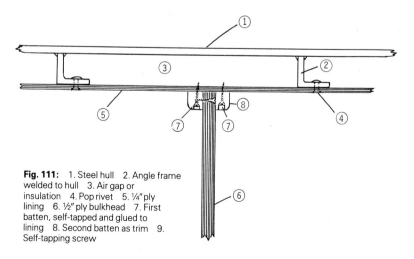

Fig. 111:   1. Steel hull   2. Angle frame welded to hull   3. Air gap or insulation   4. Pop rivet   5. ¼" ply lining   6. ½" ply bulkhead   7. First batten, self-tapped and glued to lining   8. Second batten as trim   9. Self-tapping screw

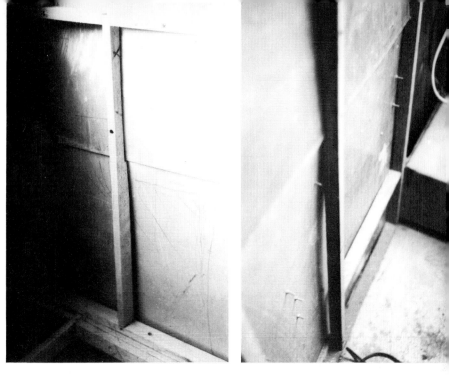

71, 72 & 73: Battens self-tapped into a distorted steel bulkhead to achieve a smooth lining

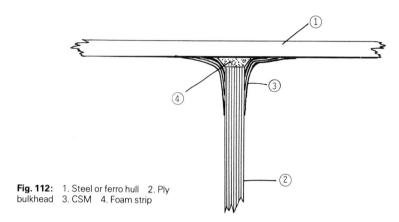

Fig. 112:   1. Steel or ferro hull   2. Ply bulkhead   3. CSM   4. Foam strip

It is also accepted practice to glass bulkheads into both steel and ferro hulls, as one would with a GRP hull, provided the necessary preparation is carried out regarding grease, dust and scoring the surface (steel). To save distortion in both materials, the bulkheads are usually bedded on a foam pad (*see* Fig. 112).

Lugs, webs or angle frames usually provide obvious fixings for main bulkheads; some different types are shown in Figs 113, 114 and 115 for ferro, and Fig. 116 shows the usual type found in steel or alloy boats.

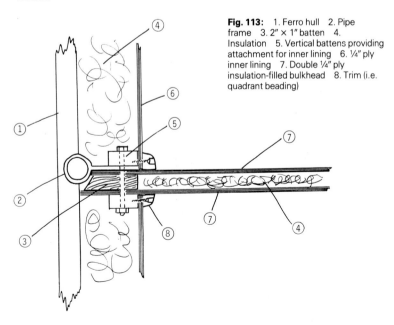

Fig. 113:   1. Ferro hull   2. Pipe frame   3. 2″ × 1″ batten   4. Insulation   5. Vertical battens providing attachment for inner lining   6. ¼″ ply inner lining   7. Double ¼″ ply insulation-filled bulkhead   8. Trim (i.e. quadrant beading)

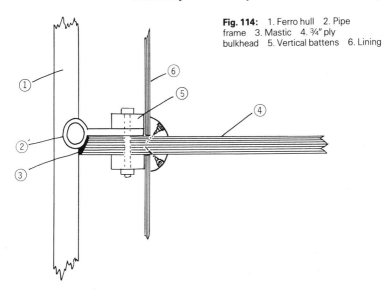

Fig. 114: 1. Ferro hull 2. Pipe frame 3. Mastic 4. ¾″ ply bulkhead 5. Vertical battens 6. Lining

All the double skinned bulkheads shown are kept rigid by internal timber divisions. The addition of foam or glass wool greatly helps general insulation and noise reduction.

Special paints for steel and ferro are described in the free booklets obtainable from paint manufacturers.

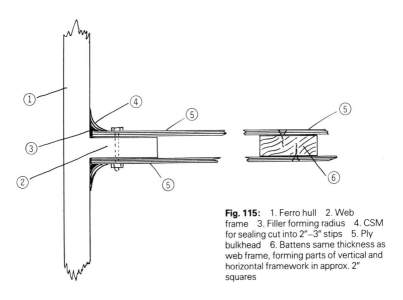

Fig. 115: 1. Ferro hull 2. Web frame 3. Filler forming radius 4. CSM for sealing cut into 2″–3″ stips 5. Ply bulkhead 6. Battens same thickness as web frame, forming parts of vertical and horizontal framework in approx. 2″ squares

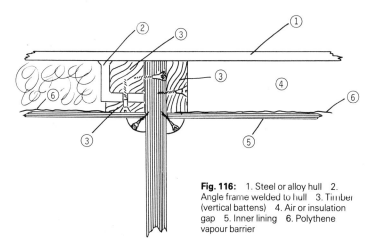

Fig. 116:   1. Steel or alloy hull   2. Angle frame welded to hull   3. Timber (vertical battens)   4. Air or insulation gap   5. Inner lining   6. Polythene vapour barrier

With steel especially, really good insulation for the hull and super-structure is necessary to avoid condensation, and where glass wool is used, a vapour barrier of polythene (*see* Fig. 116) will prevent it from absorbing too much humidity.

Cork compound and other decking materials provide good protection from chipping or scratching, and details of the necessary adhesives, if not supplied with the material, can be obtained from Bostik (*see* Appendix for address).

24 · Sea trials

This final section will be more or less a matter of course for anyone who is already an experienced sailor, but for those who are going out of the harbour for the first time, a few tips might be helpful.

I am presuming the engine trials, dealt with in a previous chapter, have been carried out successfully, and any resulting snags rectified.

There is no denying that sea trials are common sense, given time to think, but going to sea for the first time in your own boat is a very exciting occasion, and it is, I can assure you personally, very easy to overlook things in the heat of the moment.

At the risk of sounding boring, no sea trip, let alone the first one, should be undertaken lackadaisically. No aircraft ever takes off without pilot and co-pilot running a check of all essential systems, and this is a very good habit to adopt with boats, where the safety aspect is just as important.

Firstly, you must plan for the worst. Make sure you have all the necessary safety equipment, three of the most important items being life jackets for each crew member, a dinghy, inflatable or otherwise, and an anchor with plenty of chain or rope or both, securely fastened below! Indeed, everything below decks must be secured. Even in calm conditions most harbour entrances have a submerged bar which disturbs the water above it, and one good twitch can reduce a poorly stowed cabin to chaos.

Having carried out the usual checks of oil and water levels, opened the sea-cock for the cooling water if necessary and turned on the fuel, the engine may be started.

While it is warming up is a good time to complete a circuit of the deck, ensuring the anchor is secured and that at least one fore and one aft mooring line is coiled ready for use should you be leaving the permanent ones behind. If you have to go through a lock to attain the outer harbour, fenders should be secured strategically and laid on deck ready for use when required.

Your method of casting off may depend on the current, wind and how much help you have. If the wind is blowing directly across your heading, and there is little space between you and the next hazard or moored boat to leeward, confidence will be needed to accelerate quickly and firmly to gain steerage way as soon as possible. Hesitation will mean a sideways drift that could prove embarrassing.

Once out in clear water with some elbow room, try a few man-oeuvres ahead and astern to check that the steering and reverse gear work effectively. Some single-screw boats, especially those with wide transoms, are difficult to steer astern, so quite a bit of practice will be needed to work out the natural bias imposed by the propeller, and how to use it to advantage.

Don't try to be too ambitious on your first time out, and if you can stay in sheltered water, so much the better. Running for the first time can reveal propshaft misalignment that could cause a few leaks around the gland and numerous other minor problems which can be easily sorted out when you are back securely on your mooring, but not so easily in even a gently heaving sea.

Returning to the mooring can be fraught with difficulty in crowded conditions, making it necessary to maintain enough power for steerage whilst remembering that you have no brakes, apart from reverse gear. Motor boats with one or two powerful engines usually stop readily with a quick burst astern, but sailing boats with small auxiliaries often carry on almost unchecked. Your practice manoeuvres will have warned you if this is the case.

Getting a line ashore can be a tricky operation, but nevertheless necessary to accomplish quite quickly. Never be too proud to accept the co-operation of someone standing on the jetty, pontoon etc., especially in awkward, windy conditions. On the other hand, there may be no help on hand, so have a boat-hook at the ready to hold the boat in, preferably amidships, or to hook your permanent lines back to the boat to secure them. Start celebrating *after* the boat is well tied up with due allowance for tidal rise and fall.

Appendix:
Useful suppliers

Aquadrive—*see* Halyard Marine Ltd
Adhesives—*see* Bostik
    Ciba Geigy
    Evode
    Expandite Ltd
Aquamarine (UK) Ltd,
    381 Shirley Road,
    Southampton,
    Hampshire
    509 1HB
Architectural & Marine Aluminium Co.
    Ltd,
    56 Bancrofts Road,
    South Woodham Ferrers,
    Essex.

Barton Abrasives Ltd, (Ballast-Pak)
    George Henry Road, off Eagle Lane,
    Great Bridge,
    Tipton,
    West Midlands
    DY4 7BS
Bilge Pumps—*see* Henderson Pumps Ltd
    Munster Simms Engineering Ltd
Bostik Ltd,
    Consumer Products Division,
    Leicester,
    LE4 6BW
Bowman Boats (Mast Kits),
    54 Beacon Road,
    Chatham,
    Kent.
E. J. Bowman (Birmingham) Ltd,
    Cooling Equipment,
    Chester Street,
    Birmingham
    B6 4AP

British Waterways Board,
    Melbury House,
    Melbury Terrace,
    London NW1 6JX
Bukh Diesels,
South Western Marine Factors Ltd,
    43 Pottery Road,
    Parkstone,
    Poole,
    Dorset.

Calor Gas Ltd,
    Calor House,
    Windsor Road,
    Slough,
    Buckinghamshire
    SL1 2EQ
Calorifiers—*see* Golden Arrow Marine
    Ltd
Ciba Geigy Adhesives,
    Duxford,
    Cambridgeshire.
Circuit Marine—*see* Peter Smailes
Cleghorn Waring (Jabsco Pumps) Ltd,
    9–15 Hitchin Street,
    Baldock,
    Hertfordshire
Control Cables—*see* Morse Teleflex

Delta Marine Ltd, (Sterngear)
    70 Warwick Street,
    Birmingham
    B12 0NH

Dow Chemicals,
Fleximent Ltd,
Wintersells Road,
Byfleet,
Weybridge,
Surrey.
M. G. Duff Ltd,
Chichester Yacht Basin,
Birdham,
Sussex

Electrics—*see* Lucas Marine Ltd
Peter Smailes Circuit Marine
Enfieldz Drives,
Somerton Works,
Cowes,
Isle of Wight.
Essex Aluminium, (Windows and Hatch-
es)
Hall Road,
Southminster,
Essex
CMO 7EL
Evode Ltd,
Common Road,
Stafford,
ST16 3EH
Expandite Ltd,
Western Road,
Bracknell,
Berkshire.

Golden Arrow Marine Ltd,
Estate Road,
Newhaven,
East Sussex
BN9 0AL
GRP Products—*see* Martins Plastics Ltd
Strand Glassfibre

Halyard Marine Ltd (Aquadrive),
Gaines House,
Brentway,
Brentford,
Middlesex
TW8 8ES
Hatches—*see* Architectural & Marine
Aluminium Co. Ltd
Heat Exchangers—*see* Golden Arrow
Marine Ltd
E. J. Bowman (Birmingham) Ltd
Henderson Pumps Ltd,
38 Medina Road,
Cowes,
Isle of Wight.

Hulls—*see* Sadler Yachts Ltd
Tyler Mouldings Ltd
Hydraulic Drive,
H.A.P. Hydraulics Ltd,
For Road,
Lingside Industrial Estate,
Littlehampton,
Sussex.

International Paints,
24–30 Canute Road,
Southampton,
Hampshire.
I.T.T. Fluid Handling Ltd,
Belcon Industrial Estate,
Bingley Road,
Hoddesdon,
Hertfordshire
EN11 0BLL

Jabsco Pumps—*see* Cleghorn Waring

Keel Coolers—*see* Golden Arrow Marine
Ltd

Lingard Flexible Tanks,
Westminster Road,
Wareham,
Dorset
BH20 4SP
Lucas Marine Ltd,
Frimley Road,
Camberley,
Surrey
GU16 5EU

Martins Plastics Ltd,
45 Sprowston Road,
Norwich,
Norfolk
NR3 4QJ
Mast Kits—*see* Bowman Boats
Morse Teleflex Controls,
South Western Marine Factors Ltd,
5–7 Uddens Trading Estate,
Wimborne,
Dorset
BH21 7LF
Munster Simms Engineering Ltd,
(Whale Pumps)
Old Belfast Road,
Bangor,
Northern Ireland
BT19 1LT

T. Norris (Industries) Ltd, (Engines and
Equipment)
6 Wood Lane,
Isleworth,
Middlesex
TW7 5ER
Norseman Rigging Terminals,
Norseman Products,
John Shaw Ltd,
Sandy Lane,
Worksop,
Nottinghamshire
S80 3ES

Peter Smailes Circuit Marine,
2 Bramble Road,
Southsea,
Hampshire
Po4 oDT
Pressure Water Systems—*see* Cleghorn
Waring
I.T.T. Fluid Handling Ltd
Aquamarine (UK) Ltd

Sadler Yachts Ltd,
29–31 Dawkins Road,
Hamworthy,
Poole,
Dorset.

Scorpion Aluminium Products Ltd,
(Windows and Hatches)
Unit 4, Springfield Industrial Estate,
Springfield Road,
Burnham on Crouch,
Essex.
Sealers—*see* Bostik Ltd
Expandite Ltd
Dow Chemicals
Strand Glassfibre,
Brentway Trading Estate,
Brentford,
Middlesex
TW8 8ER

Thames Water Authority,
Nugent House,
Vastern Road,
Reading,
Berkshire.
Toilets—*see* I.T.T. Fluid Handling Ltd
Golden Arrow Marine Ltd
Tyler Mouldings Ltd,
56–58 Morley Road,
Tonbridge,
Kent
TN9 1RP

Windows—*see* Architectural & Marine
Aluminium Co. Ltd

Index

012855033

READERS WORKSHOPS

BRIDGING LITERATURE AND LITERACY

.IVERPOOL HOPE UNIVERSITY
THE SHEPPARD - WORLOCK LIBRA

Stories from teachers
and their classrooms

Edited by Terry MacKenzie

IRWIN PUBLISHING
Toronto, Canada

Copyright ©1992 by Irwin Publishing

ISBN 0–7725-1931–5

Canadian Cataloguing in Publication Data

Main entry under title:

Readers' workshops

Includes bibliographical references.
ISBN 0–7725–1931–5

1. Reading (Elementary).   2. Reading (Secondary).
3. Literature — Study and teaching.   4. Literacy
programs.   I. MacKenzie, Terry, 1946–

LB1573.R43 1992   428.4'07   C92–093698–9

No part of this book may be reproduced or
transmitted in any form or by any means,
electronic or mechanical, including photocopy,
recording or any information storage and retrieval
system now known or to be invented, without
permission in writing from the publisher, except
by a reviewer who wishes to quote brief passages in
connection with a review written for inclusion in a
magazine, newspaper, or broadcast.

Cover design by Pronk&Associates
Text design by Pronk&Associates
Typeset by Pronk&Associates
Printed in Canada by The Alger Press Limited

1   2   3   4   5   AP   96   95   94   93   92

Published by
Irwin Publishing
1800 Steeles Avenue West
Concord, Ontario
L4K 2P3